Supporting Wellb
through Gender-Inclusive
Practices

Gender is a broad and complex concept, the impact of which can start even before a baby is born. It can be a source of restriction, but it is also a source of joy, and early years practitioners have a unique opportunity to empower new generations by creating gender-inclusive environments where children feel confident and, above all, happy.

This accessible and practical guide provides meaningful advice on how to improve and promote gender inclusion and wellbeing in early years settings. Chapters cover key areas, from gendered language and gender-inclusive environments to trans and non-binary childhoods, and encourage practitioners to reflect deeply on the way gender has impacted their own lives. The book provides:

- An overview and analysis of current guidance around gender equality and how this is integral to best practice.
- Real-world practical tips and strategies that can be introduced right away, including advice for working effectively with parents.
- Book recommendations for settings and consideration of the language used in fairy tales and nursery rhymes, as well as signposting to further learning for practitioners.
- Guidance on creating gender-inclusive environments and making space for children to play around and make choices based on what brings them joy.
- Reflection points, practitioner reflections, and case studies to bring theory to life.

The early years presents the perfect time to encourage the exploration of identity as part of play, and the book enables practitioners to actively engage with this, to recognise and celebrate individuality, and to promote social, emotional, and mental wellbeing. This refreshing guide empowers practitioners to push boundaries in their setting to enable and maximise a positive approach to gender in practice. It is essential reading for all early years practitioners, as well as childminders and early childhood students.

Fifi Benham is an early years practitioner and writer specialising in disability and LGBTQ+ inclusion. They have eight years of in-setting experience, including being deputy manager, safeguarding lead, and SENDCo.

Little Minds Matter
Promoting Social and Emotional Wellbeing in the Early Years
Series Advisor: Sonia Mainstone-Cotton

The *Little Minds Matter* series promotes best practice for integrating social and emotional health and wellbeing into the early years setting. It introduces practitioners to a wealth of activities and resources to support them in each key area: from providing access to ideas for unstructured, imaginative outdoor play; activities to create a sense of belonging and form positive identities; and, importantly, strategies to encourage early years professionals to create a workplace that positively contributes to their own wellbeing, as well as the quality of their provision. The *Little Minds Matter* series ensures that practitioners have the tools they need to support every child.

Building Positive Relationships in the Early Years
Conversations to Empower Children, Professionals, Families and Communities
Sonia Mainstone-Cotton and Jamel Carly Campbell

Developing Child-Centred Practice for Safeguarding and Child Protection
Strategies for Every Early Years Setting
Rachel Buckler

Little Brains Matter
A Practical Guide to Brain Development and Neuroscience in Early Childhood
Debbie Garvey

Creativity and Wellbeing in the Early Years
Practical Ideas and Activities for Young Children
Sonia Mainstone-Cotton

Anti-Racist Practice in the Early Years
A Holistic Framework for the Wellbeing of All Children
Valerie Daniel

Speech, Language and Communication for Healthy Little Minds
Practical Ideas to Promote Communication for Wellbeing in the Early Years
Becky Poulter Jewson and Rebeca Skinner

Promoting Physical Development and Activity in Early Childhood
Practical Ideas for Early Years Settings
Jackie Musgrave, Jane Dorrian, Joanne Josephidou, Ben Langdown and Lucy Rodriguez Leon

Supporting Wellbeing through Gender-Inclusive Practices
A Practical Guide for Early Years Educators
Fifi Benham

Supporting Wellbeing through Gender-Inclusive Practices

A Practical Guide for Early Years Educators

Fifi Benham

Routledge
Taylor & Francis Group

LONDON AND NEW YORK

Designed cover image: The Children of Sparkles Pre-school

First published 2025
by Routledge
4 Park Square, Milton Park, Abingdon, Oxon OX14 4RN

and by Routledge
605 Third Avenue, New York, NY 10158

Routledge is an imprint of the Taylor & Francis Group, an informa business

British Library Cataloguing-in-Publication Data
A catalogue record for this book is available from the British Library

ISBN: 978-1-032-36785-9 (hbk)
ISBN: 978-1-032-36784-2 (pbk)
ISBN: 978-1-003-33378-4 (ebk)

DOI: 10.4324/b23179

Typeset in Optima
by Deanta Global Publishing Services, Chennai, India

Contents

Foreword

This latest book in our *Little Minds Matter* series is on the subject of how we support wellbeing through gender-inclusive practice. I am so pleased we have this book in our series at this current time when there is much debate and conversation about this area; it feels very timely to have a book offering us practical and calm guidance and support.

The joy of this book is how practical and readable it is. Fifi guides us through this subject with sensitivity and gentleness, whilst offering many ideas and suggestions. They weave through examples from their own practice, and from others, and offer case studies for us to reflect on. Throughout the book Fifi helps us understand the terminology and theory in an accessible way, to think about the language we use with children, and offer guidance on how we might tweak this. The book also considers how we can work with adults who may have concerns, reservations, and fears.

Wellbeing is at the heart of this book. This may sound obvious as our series focuses upon wellbeing, but Fifi has continued to weave in this golden thread throughout, helping us all to understand how gender-inclusive practice is such a vital part of supporting a child's wellbeing.

I came away with many new ideas, resources, and books I can use. I felt I had some knowledge in this area, but finished the book feeling a lot more informed and equipped. This is a book which will be useful for every early years setting. It will be an excellent book to use as part of CPD practice and team conversations and discussions, and it is a book for early years students to read at the start of their early careers.

Sonia Mainstone-Cotton
Series Advisor
May 2024

Acknowledgements

Thank you to Sparkles Pre-school for providing the images for this book, and to the children of Sparkles for their wonderful artwork.

Introduction

Introduction

There is increasing awareness of the need to strive for inclusive practice in the early years but often this can be held back by nervousness or uncertainty about how to go about that. This book will help both in providing a greater understanding of what it means to be inclusive and why it is essential in supporting children's wellbeing. There are case studies, practical ideas, and contributions from a range of practitioners, parents, and people with lived experience of gender nonconformity to ensure a range of relevant voices are heard.

Supporting children's wellbeing is at the heart of all we do as early years practitioners. It is present on all levels from our legal duty of care to individual setting policies. Supporting wellbeing means recognising existing barriers and sources of potential harm. Gender is often treated as an inescapable set of rules and boundaries that dictate our skills, struggles, and opportunities. As early years practitioners we have a unique opportunity to help shift perception so that newer generations don't have to feel limited or boxed in by gender, but instead are free to play, explore, and dream.

DOI: 10.4324/b23179-1

Inclusive practice

In educational settings, we must uphold the Equality Act 2010, which lists sex and gender reassignment as protected characteristics. This means we have a duty to eliminate discrimination, advance equality of opportunity, and foster good relations between people who share those protected characteristics and people who do not. In order to achieve this it's essential we challenge both our own perceptions of gender and the culture surrounding gendered play across the sector to centre inclusion and overcome potential barriers caused by reinforcement of "traditional" gender roles.

We are supposed to be helping prepare children to thrive in the world, and that includes instilling a sense of acceptance and respect for the increasingly diverse communities children will be growing up in. Being able to exist peacefully alongside people whose identities differ significantly from our own is essential to our wellbeing.

Regardless of any intent to cause harm, we are all subject to adopting biases that can be reflected in our practice. This means we may not be giving all children the same access to opportunities or forming positive relationships with children whose protected characteristics differ from our own. The only way to move past this is active self-reflection and seeking necessary education and professional development to eliminate potentially harmful practices.

The idea of "inclusion" is that all children feel represented and valued and are presented with the same level of opportunity and engagement regardless of identifiers including, but not limited to, gender, sexuality, race, religion, class or disability. This is often interpreted as treating everyone the same, but many recognise that this approach doesn't take into account the very real impact of marginalisation and as such does not truly result in equality of opportunity. This is why many people prefer to strive for "equity" as this specifically relates to fairness and justice rather than demanding a totally identical approach for all.

Gender-inclusive practice means that the expansive nature of gender is understood, and active efforts are made to ensure children do not see gender as a dividing or limiting factor. A culture is created wherein practitioners are able to challenge each other, children, and their families to ensure sexism and transphobia are not being reinforced.

Defining gender

Gender is defined and understood in a vast range of ways depending on community, location, and politics amongst a range of other factors. The use of "gender" throughout this book refers to the system of social and material norms, behaviours, and expectations of distinct roles within society that mark people as different in socially significant ways (Lorber, 1994; Ridgeway and Smith-Lovin, 1999; Connell and Pearse, 2014).

Children's socialisation differs based on their assigned sex from birth. Sometimes, even prior to birth, gender can impact the clothes and toys bought as well as the decoration of the nursery in preparation. Throughout childhood, children absorb messaging about what it means to be a certain gender and develop a sense of gender identity. People whose gender identity aligns with expectations based on their assigned sex are typically referred to as cisgender, whilst people whose identity does not align with expectations based on assigned sex are typically referred to as transgender, often used as an umbrella term encompassing a range of gender nonconformity.

The external societal constructs involved in gender mean that there is inevitably an element of performance to gender, as we replicate or diverge from expectations. The term "gender performativity" was coined by Judith Butler (1993) to explain the process of projecting gender in our behaviours and expression.

Throughout history, there have always been people who have challenged the notion of gender in a range of ways (politically, socially, in performance) yet, as this is often followed by a period of stricter enforcement of norms both legally and socially, challenging gender is always treated as if it's a new, out-there concept.

We are living in a period of increased visibility of the transgender community. The Women and Equalities Select Committee's (2016) report on "Transgender Equality" recognised the "complex and extensive hierarchy of issues that need to be addressed" to further trans rights, and laid out the ways the Equality Act 2010 is insufficient in protecting trans people. Very few of the recommendations made in the report have been put into practice and, in fact, there are efforts to roll back existing protections despite the majority response to the report at the time being positive.

Wellbeing

There are many aspects to wellbeing, and it is our role as early years practitioners to support children's wellbeing holistically. The word "wellbeing" isn't easily defined as a singular thing but rather a complex concept that means different things to different people. Ultimately as practitioners, supporting wellbeing includes engaging positively with children; recognising risk factors to social, emotional, and mental health; and minimising potential harm.

The concept of wellbeing as a set of scales, with one side being risk factors and the other being protective factors, was put forth by Dodge et al. (2012). They explained that "stable wellbeing is when individuals have the psychological, social and physical resources they need to meet a particular psychological, social or physical challenge. When individuals have more challenges than resources, the (scales) dip, along with their wellbeing and vice versa". This means we need to consider what protective factors for children may be and how to maximise them in our practice. Fostering positive relationships, giving children knowledge and understanding, and providing emotional support can contribute to wellbeing as protective factors. It is not always possible to achieve balance, and risk factors to wellbeing will always exist, but by recognising imbalance we can help consider how we may alleviate risk and offer protection.

There are many ways gender can impact wellbeing. The expectations set by traditional gender roles can make people feel very restricted and create fear around not fitting into very narrow ideals. When children are absorbing messages about how someone of their gender should look and behave this causes pressure to conform and failing to do so can cause significant distress.

In a gender-inclusive environment, gender can have a positive impact on wellbeing. When gender is recognised as subjective and freely explorable the expectation to meet certain definitions is removed. Gender becomes de-emphasised as one facet of identity that shouldn't set any limitations on interests or aspirations. This results in gender being able to be a source of affirmation and self-confidence.

REFLECTIVE PRACTICE

As early years practitioners we need to be continuously reflecting on our practice and adapting in response to those reflections. This is important not only in striving to achieve best practice but also in checking in with our own wellbeing and how we feel about the work we do. However, the busyness of the job doesn't lend itself well to having time and space to reflect independently. We have to respond to what's happening in the moment and this can mean opportunities to improve get missed, or that we fixate on things we could have done differently without examining why we respond in certain ways.

The purpose of reflection points throughout this book is not to provide homework but to prompt introspection in a way that's meaningful to you. The aim is to encourage curiosity and lead to improved practice by refocusing on things within our control. There's no shame in recognising aspects of our own practice that could be better. We are all trying to do our best with the knowledge and resources we have, and when we strive to expand our learning and continued professional development we increase our capacity to achieve even better practice.

Language

Conscious effort has been made to reflect community preference in language use throughout this book when referencing gender as well as other minoritised communities. However, language preferences have always been something that shifts over time in response to societal progress and increased awareness. This is a positive thing overall, but may mean texts contain outdated terminology even if best practice was followed at the time of writing. Language surrounding identity can also be deeply personal, meaning terms that one person finds affirming another person may find offensive.

Childcare vs education

Early years often gets forgotten about as a stage of education in favour of being viewed as just somewhere for parents and carers to put their children for a bit so they can get back to work. For this reason, those working within early years emphasise that our sector's purpose is early childhood education. Good quality provision in early years makes a significant difference to children's achievements throughout and beyond further education, yet we are chronically underfunded and undervalued.

It is necessary to continue to push for broader recognition that we are educators. However, in many ways I feel that actually all stages of education would benefit from increased focus on caring alongside teaching. Whilst it's true the term "childcare" has negative implications in it's dismissal of the complexity of our jobs, total rejection of the word "care" also overlooks a large part of what we provide. It is through truly caring about children and their futures that we form connections and work towards best practice.

Current context

It is important to emphasise this is being written in the UK at a particularly worrying point in time for trans rights both here and overseas. Despite the initial push being from a very small number of loud voices, many individuals and organisations in positions of significant political power have made statements which explicitly attack trans rights (Stonewall, 2023; TransActual, 2024; Hansford, 2024; Good Law Project, 2024).

This wave of attacks also seeks to set far more rigid definitions of two gender roles into legislation, which ultimately harms all people and would be a huge step backwards in terms of equal rights. People have fought hard to reduce the impact of gender on equality of opportunity yet that risks being undone for the sake of punishing a small marginalised community.

This makes the creation of resources which support gender inclusion and, by extension, trans liberation, all the more essential so that we may forge a path through this and ensure future generations are not having to defend their existence in this way.

Conclusion

Conversations around gender, inclusion, and wellbeing, and what those concepts mean in the context of the early years, are ongoing and currently gaining a lot of attention. As such, it's essential these topics are a focus of learning and professional development for practitioners in order that we make full use of this opportunity to push for positive change. This book will provide information, ideas, and opportunities for reflection with the aim of improving practitioners' confidence in implementing gender-inclusive practice.

References

Butler, J. (1993) *Bodies That Matter: On the Discursive Limits of "Sex"*. London: Routledge.

Connell, R. and Pearse, R. (2014) *Gender: In World Perspective*. Cambridge: Polity Press.

Dodge, R., Daly, A., Huyton, J. and Sanders, L. (2012) "The challenge of defining wellbeing". *International Journal of Wellbeing*, 2(3), 222–235. doi:10.5502/ijw.v2i3.4

Good Law Project (2024) "Labour defends tory trans healthcare ban that will have a grave impact on young lives". https://goodlawproject

.org/update/labour-defends-tory-trans-healthcare-ban-that-will-have-a-grave-impact-on-young-lives/

Hansford, A (2024) "Keir Starmer and Rishi Sunak's views on trans rights: What's the difference". https://www.thepinknews.com/2024/06/27/rishi-sunak-keir-starmer-trans-rights/

Lorber, J. (1994) *Paradoxes of Gender*. New Haven, CT: Yale University Press.

Ridgeway, C. L., and Smith-Lovin, L. (1999) "The gender system and interaction". *Annual Review of Sociology*, 25, 191–216.

Stonewall (2023) "EHRC 'actively harming' trans people, ignoring international recommendations, charities warn". https://www.stonewall.org.uk/about-us/news/ehrc-'actively-harming'-trans-people-ignoring-international-recommendations-charities

TransActual (2024) "Statement on Wes streeting's comments about trans-specific hospital wards". https://transactual.org.uk/blog/2024/01/30/statement-on-wes-streetings-comments-about-trans-specific-hospital-wards/

Women and Equalities Committee (2016) "Transgender equality: First report of session 2015–16". https://publications.parliament.uk/pa/cm201516/cmselect/cmwomeq/390/390.pdf

Gender-inclusive environments

Gender-inclusive environments

Often in the early years and education sectors, people talk about creating a "gender-neutral" environment. Whilst the intention behind this is positive, striving for an environment that centres inclusion over neutrality provides a stronger foundation for children to thrive in their individuality. Regardless of individual experience, we as practitioners must acknowledge the way society's binary idea of gender attempts to dictate different aspects of life. Often, even before a baby is born, their bedroom is decorated in either pink or blue based on their assigned sex. The gender binary then continues to be everywhere: toys, clothing, adverts, TV shows, books, magazines, etc. This means we could never truly create a gender neutral environment because our settings exist in the context of a world that genders almost everything. Children will have already absorbed ideas about what is and isn't for them and so even though we might say that we'll let anyone play with anything, the types and designs of our resources often attach to gender. By shifting focus to a gender-inclusive environment, we acknowledge that many of the resources we have are not neutral, and that is okay as long as we know how to encourage children to explore and follow their interests. It is up to educators to model and encourage exploring resources indiscriminately and developing individual preferences which aren't dictated by gender.

DOI: 10.4324/b23179-2

Many practitioners who talk about gender neutrality seem to almost exclusively mean that they won't stop boys from wearing dresses or pushing prams. This is a passive process, with a limited view of inclusion. If we shift our aim to creating a gender-inclusive environment, we can focus on the active learning and changes needed in order to recognise and value gender identity, without centring outdated binary gender norms.

Small world play

Inanimate objects can't truly have a gender, but they can mimic gender expression. This means that elements of dolls such as clothing, hair length, and body types need to be varied in every set and this extends beyond nuclear family sets for doll houses. Any small world play which has dolls needs variance in gender expression, race, and disabilities in order to teach children that their aspirations shouldn't be dependent on these factors.

Small world play is also a space the frequently divides children based on gender. Stereotypes certainly exist surrounding who might play with a train set versus a dolls' house or dinosaurs versus fairies. One way to challenge this is by combining different small world sets. For example, maybe one day the dolls' houses are full of dinosaurs or another day the train set is providing transport for fairies. This is a great way to keep things interesting and to draw more people in without needing entirely new resources.

Small world toys can also be used to draw children into activities they wouldn't normally engage with. In one setting, there were some children who wanted to always play with cars and seemed uninterested in other activities. In response, practitioners considered how cars can be used in other areas including sensory play, painting with cars, attaching pens to cars, and creating a numbered car park.

Figure 2.1 A Tuff tray activity with a spiral of different colours of paint with cars dotted along the spiral and paintbrushes.

 REFLECTION POINT

Look around your early years setting/space. Are there areas or resources that seem to only be drawing in children of one gender? We have a duty to fulfil the Early Years Foundation Stage (EYFS), and part of that will mean making all areas appealing to everyone, otherwise we risk hindering children's progress. Carrying out an observation of where children go in the setting and their gender can help identify areas that may need re-examining.

It could also be useful to involve the children as a follow-up to these observations. Asking children questions such as "which area of the room do you like the most?" and "why is that?" could provide insight that will help you make all areas more inviting to all children.

One way you could incorporate this as a regular part of practice is by using photographs of different areas and having children place a photo of themselves in their favourite area. When you have made changes you could repeat the activity to see if those changes had the intended impact.

Figure 2.2 A wooden dolls' house on a mat with a patch of grass. There is a dragon on the roof and dinosaurs inside the dolls' house and on the mat.

Overall environment

Different early years settings will have varying abilities to decorate their space. Whether you have to pack away every day or have complete control over your space, there are lots of different ways to create an inviting early years environment, and as such no singular "right" way to go about it.

Often when we think of making a space gender inclusive there's a tendency to steer away from particular colours. Cordelia Fine (2011) observed, "So thoroughly have these preferences become ingrained that psychologists and journalists now speculate on the genetic and evolutionary origins of gendered colour preferences that are little more than fifty years old". Claiming an innate, gendered preference is unfounded so avoiding assumptions about what girls and boys might like is essential. For example, if children have different coloured pegs then it's absolutely important not to use gender as the colour decider. Avoidance of pink and blue in these contexts isn't necessarily a negative; as mentioned above, children will have absorbed messages about what things that are for boys and what things for girls look like, and colour is certainly a part of that. This has the potential to lead to children limiting themselves. For example, if all of your prams and cots and dolls' clothes are pink, some boys may not feel they are being invited to play with them.

Many settings are working towards having fewer plastic resources, which often means replacing them with wooden toys that don't feature the same bright colours as their plastic counterparts. Settings that make heavier use of found objects too will likely have less visually gendered items. This is to say that it's possible to combine efforts to create a more gender-inclusive space with a broader re-examination of resources for environmental and pedagogical reasons.

Figure 2.3 Large wooden blocks of varying lengths with holes to use as connectors are piled up together. Different sized pine cones have been put into the holes.

14

REFLECTION POINT

Do you have a favourite area of your setting? If you do, consider what that area looks like or the activities it contains and why you feel drawn to it. Are there aspects of that area that could be brought over to other parts of the setting that would make exploring different areas more appealing?

Are there parts of the setting you dislike or tend to avoid? If there are, consider what may be making them seem uninviting to you, as it's likely these could also be making certain children dislike them too. Focus on changes that you can make, whether that's easy things like moving a certain activity to the garden or whether that needs more time and investment like an overhaul of resources.

The workforce

There's no getting around the fact that the majority of early years practitioners are women and there are multiple reasons for this. Outdated ideas about different genders having a specific set of shared, innate skills are still very present in a lot of sectors and change is slow. In the 2018 Labour Force Survey it was found that 92.6% of childcare workers were women.

Calls for more men in the early years risk advancing essentialist notions of masculinity (Tembo, 2021). Diversifying the workforce calls for broader recognition of gender as expansive as well as how gender relates to other aspects of identity. The history of women only being able to access professions involving care also complicates the divide and how to rectify it in the early years sector. We cannot solely focus on levelling gender divides that were initially caused by limitations of opportunity without seeking to make significant changes to industries that are difficult to break into for anyone other than men.

Ultimately, the best way to begin to correct the disproportionate gender divides is to continue and expand efforts to show children that gender shouldn't matter in career paths. We have a responsibility as early years practitioners to instil a belief that all genders are capable of any job.

PRACTITIONER REFLECTION – DAVID CAHN

Despite the mountains of evidence that show how vital positive relationships, play, and healthy environments are for young children's development, our world still operates under the patriarchal idea that *all* women are "natural caregivers", so basically the workforce is made up of "girls who can't get real jobs". Politicians may pay lip service to the importance of early years education, but they never back it up in their policies and we all know the low perceived status of this work in our hearts.

The flipside of the idea that "all women are natural caregivers' is that men simply aren't, and the few men who work in early years care and education are weirdos, and possibly even threats to people's children.

If our sector was a ship, it has been slowly sinking for decades. Whilst I can empathise with the sentiment of "getting more men in early years" it is honestly the equivalent of rearranging the deck chairs on the Titanic. Of course I want to shatter the idea that men can't or don't know how to care, but we need to push for something far more reaching than simply changing the demographics of our – over-stretched, underpaid, practically entirely female – workforce. In fact, I feel it can often serve as a convenient distraction from the real fundamental issues facing our sector.

I can honestly empathise! The ways capitalism, patriarchy, and white supremacy hold our sector back can be overwhelming to think about. They would require a true revolution in our shared understanding of the importance of caring labour – whether for the young, elderly, or disabled – as an essential part of our shared humanity and success as a species. I have no solutions or easy answers but like the generic advice we can be tempted to give children when faced with a problem, I am "using my words".

Current guidance

Development Matters (2021) states in the key features of effective practice that "all children deserve to have an equal chance of success". This is relevant in that heteronormativity perpetuates outdated concepts of which skills and jobs are suited to which gender. In order for children to have an equal chance of success, practitioners must create a space where exploration of different futures is not restricted in this way.

Development Matters guidance on Understanding the World includes avoiding "songs which include gender, cultural or racial stereotypes". Gender stereotypes in particular relate to heteronormativity as, in rhymes or songs for young children, they will often refer to mummies and daddies doing different activities or filling different roles.

The guidance also includes supporting children's understanding and exploration of people's differences using "materials which confront gender stereotypes". This makes it clear that best practice goes beyond not just perpetuating stereotypes but necessitates actively confronting them.

Birth to 5 Matters (2021) also has a section on inclusive practice and equality, which explains how gender stereotypes can limit children's potential. Specific emphasis is placed on ensuring children see themselves and their families represented.

An example of the ways this document builds upon guidance set out in Development Matters is that Birth to 5 advises that our resources must "avoid stereotypical depictions of people based on gender and sexual orientation'. This is a significant consideration when creating a gender-inclusive environment as it shows recognition of the potential harm of stereotypes relating to gender and sexuality. Often stereotypes surrounding sexuality tie into gender in that it's assumed the queer community is essentially feminine men and masculine women rather than a community that encompasses an expansive range of gender expression and identity.

It is also stated in Birth to 5 Matters (2021) that "practitioners should share their willingness to challenge stereotypes and misunderstandings'. This promotes individual practitioners taking responsibility for actively addressing these issues as they arise. Although the statement is not specific to any one type of stereotype, this guidance can be applied as a willingness to challenge statements or actions which reinforce gender stereotypes.

Giving children control over their environment

Ask children what they want to see displayed in their setting. If they bring you something and ask you to display it, try and say yes. Even if you just stick it on for that day, this helps validate children's control over their environment and encourages them to be proud of their work at the same time.

In my own practice with a new cohort of children we would get a long blank piece of paper, have children choose a coloured pen, and ask them to draw a picture themselves. It's best to avoid steering them beyond so that children can interpret your prompt how they want to. Some children may draw recognisable people that share their features and others might draw a quick squiggle and move on.

CASE STUDY

After receiving feedback that their displays didn't feel like they were a reflection of the children, one pre-school decided to completely overhaul their existing displays with a new idea. They made a frame out of card for each child and put a label on each frame with a child's name. The children are then able to choose when they want something displayed, and it's attached with blue tac so that it's easily changeable during the day without causing any damage to the artwork. Children enjoy looking at their artwork displayed and have fun choosing what they want to go in their frame. This system also means visitors to the setting get to see a reflection of a range of crafts the children have enjoyed doing, rather than an overly curated display of a singular activity that doesn't necessarily incorporate the child's voice.

Figure 2.4 A black display board with different coloured frames. In each frame is a different piece of colourful artwork made by children.

Social environment

We need an awareness of broader societal issues to inform the way we respond to different children. Everyone will have been absorbing biases from birth. Being conscious of our own biases, as well as that of our colleagues and children, is key to better practice. A boy in your setting might have the same desire as a girl in your setting to put on a princess dress. The difference is that the girl will have seen countless people who look like her wearing clothes like that, whereas the boy could easily have seen none. This means you may need to offer different encouragement. You need to anticipate that other children or, unfortunately, staff might laugh or make a comment and be ready to intercept. Several children's films and TV programmes feature the joke where a man ends up in a dress and is humiliated and it's all hilarious. Awareness of the precious thing that is a child doing what they want despite societal or cultural expectations is essential here and we cannot nurture this without acknowledging that every child is not the same.

Advertising

Progress has been made in recent years regarding toys and resources specifically being labelled as "for boys" or "for girls". However, explicitly stating gender isn't the only way images, shops, and advertisements promote toys in a way that denotes intention for a particular gender. In a 2017 study of toy catalogues, girls were twice as likely to be shown with art and craft toys; boys were almost twice as likely to be shown with construction toys; 100% of children shown with beauty/grooming toys were girls; boys were ten times more likely to be shown with superhero-themed "action figures" and much less likely to be shown with other kinds of "small world" play; girls were more likely to be shown in dressing-up clothes, but boys got more variety. Over half the girls dressing up were shown in princess or fairy outfits, mostly in passive poses, whilst 40% of boys were shown in superhero outfits, mostly in active poses.

Consider images in your setting. It's common to have photos of children in the setting playing as part of displays and so reflecting on the content of these images and the messages they may be sending. Good practice would be to have a display of children's creations alongside images of them making them, and ensuring photos of any given activity include all genders.

It's important to consider the impact this has on children, and the steps we can take to help counter that. Some settings still have variations on "Pirates and Princesses Day". This has the potential to be very polarising and cause upset if children feel forced to wear something they don't want to. If you do have events like these, consider how to make invitations clear that the options aren't restricted by gender in both your wording choices and images so that children can see that it's okay to choose either option.

For managers, advertising your setting in a way that reflects your inclusive practice helps promote your ethos and values which will help in creating an expectation that must be upheld by the setting and supported by families. If your advertisements include images, these should feature different children engaging in a full range of activities that have typically been viewed as being "for" a specific gender. When families come to look around, promoting your inclusion policies and explaining how they are implemented means families can feel safe in the knowledge that staff will be providing the best possible care and education for all children.

Book corner

We all know the importance of reading in furthering children's development across all areas. This is why decisions about which books to have in early years settings and how to present them must be purposeful. Part of this is looking at the quantity of different genders as main characters. Whilst we want children to learn to relate to and empathise with people who are different to them, it is important that all children feel they are represented in their environment.

Beyond examining the quantity, it's just as important to examine the content of books and if they are reinforcing gender stereotypes. If all of your books with boy main characters are about exploring and adventuring but all of your books with girl main characters are about being creative, then this promotes the incorrect idea that gender dictates what you are capable of. Consider the personalities of main characters; often girls are presented as more passive and timid whilst boys are presented as confident and brave. This again can make children feel restricted by their gender and afraid to stray from what's expected of them.

Family dynamics in books are also a key consideration. Children need to know that some families have one parent, some have two dads or two mums, and some children aren't raised by their parents at all. Gender stereotypes about care and responsibility are intertwined with expectations of cisgender-heterosexual nuclear families. Furthermore, we need to have books that talk about trans identities. Ideally this will include more abstract representations of transition like *Julian Is a Mermaid*, by Jessica Love, and more literal representations like *When Aidan Became a Brother*.

Difficulties with wellbeing and mental illness currently differ based on gender, due to societal expectations of who should feel which emotion and how they should deal with that. Most settings will have books dealing with different emotions and coping mechanisms as a way to further children's personal, social, and emotional development. This is a fantastic idea but it's important to reflect on which characters are being used to explore which emotions, and make purposeful choices based on this. When it comes to books about emotions, are we seeing a range from different genders, or are we just seeing angry boys and crying girls?

Valuing play

There is a perception that boys and girls will instinctively play with different things, even now that we have largely moved past ideas about these preferences being innate. Although most practitioners will not purposefully differentiate their expectations of boys and girls, we may be pushing ideas about who should be doing what subconsciously.

Practitioners are early years settings' most important resource! As with other elements of the overall environment, we can be a positive force for supporting inclusion. Practitioners have to be willing to get involved in a range of play with a range of children. If a practitioner is engaging with roleplaying nuclear families in the home corner but avoiding superhero roleplays in the garden, this sends the message that certain types of roleplay hold less value than others. Practitioners are also essential to meeting the EYFS and maximising opportunities for learning. This means that if different groups of children are getting more attention from practitioners, not everyone is able to access the same level of education.

In addition to the education aspect, all children benefit socially and emotionally from forming connections with adults, and having fun together is one of the best ways to do that. This means practitioners have to meet children where they're at both in terms of communication and enjoyment. Child-initiated play opens up opportunities for imagination and exploration (Woods, 2017) so we must honour these with a willingness to follow the child's interests. If we try to steer things based on gendered expectations, we place limitations on what can be explored and potentially close off our ability to form connections. Equally, if we're only willing to get involved when activities appeal to us we may end up building connections with children that are sub-consciously influenced by gender, meaning certain demographics don't get to build relationships with adults in the same way as others.

PRACTITIONER REFLECTION – KIM BENHAM

When people are interviewed for an early years post they don't normally expect questions on gender or LGBTQIA+ identities which is why I now include them in my interview process. People at interview often, when asked an unexpected question, don't take the time to think out their answer so you are able to get a pretty clear idea of their attitudes and dispositions. Depending on their response my attitude and disposition kicks in too. When you ask, "If a dad asks you to not let his son play with prams and/or dress up in princess clothes, what would you say?" you can expect a number of responses. Several times candidates have replied "you can discourage them" which you can leave there if you want to. For me it's an invitation to unwrap that statement and dig deeper. Why would they discourage it? Is that the answer they thought I expected or wanted? Did they want to comply with the parent's wishes? By scratching beneath the surface you can see if you have an open-minded, diverse, fair person in front of you, or do you have somebody who has very stereotypical views that might be be non-negotiable to them and therefore not suitable for our families, especially our children?

Conclusion

Creating a gender-inclusive environment does necessitate a thorough examination of resources and willingness to make significant changes over time where resources or other aspects of the physical environment are observed to be a barrier to fully accessing the range of play and learning opportunities provided. All children deserve to feel welcome and encouraged to explore in an environment that values reflecting their interests. Avoiding enforcing gender stereotypes doesn't necessitate avoiding anything that could be considered to be designed to appeal to a specific gender but rather looking at how such things are presented and observing the impact that has on children's play. Through taking action in response to observed limitations we maximise the potential for both learning and fun in our settings.

Further learning

The "Let Toys Be Toys" campaign aims to overcome limiting children's interests by defining items as being for a particular gender. Their website https://www.lettoysbetoys.org.uk has a range of resources including some specifically aimed at early years practitioners as well as guides for parents and carers on how to challenge gender stereotypes at home and how to express concerns to early years and other educational settings that may be perpetuating stereotypes.

The teacher technology solution (TTS) group article "Learning to Play the Natural Way – the Benefits of Natural Resources" discusses ways in which natural resources can be utilised and how this helps create opportunities for fun and learning.

The Early Years Foundations Stage Forum podcast titled "Creating a gender-inclusive environment in your setting" is a discussion around the importance of gender inclusion and what that means in practice.

References

Department for Education (2021) "Development matters: Non-statutory curriculum guidance for the early years foundation stage". https://assets.publishing.service.gov.uk/government/uploads/system/uploads/attachment_data/file/914443/Development_Matters_-_Non-statutory_curriculum_guidance_for_the_early_years_foundation_stage__1_.pdf

Early Years Coalition (2021) "Birth to 5 matters: Non-statutory guidance for the early years foundation stage". https://www.birthto5matters.org.uk/

Fine, Cordelia (2011) *Delusions of Gender*. London: Icon Books Ltd, p. 208.

Let Toys Be Toys (n.d.) "Toy catalogues research: Tracking changing trends in toy catalogues". *Let Toys Be Toys*. Available at: https://www.lettoysbetoys.org.uk/research/toy-catalogues/

National Education Union (2023) "Breaking the mould". *National Education Union*. Available at: https://neu.org.uk/advice/classroom/teaching-resources/breaking-mould

Tembo, S. (2021) 'More work to do: thinking through equalities with young children in Scotland', in Palmer, S. (ed.) *Play is the Way*. 2nd ed. Paisley: CCWB Press, pp. 186-196.

https://www.anewchapterbooks.com/

Woods, Annie (2017) *Child-initiated play and learning: Planning for possibilities in the early years*. Routledge

3 | Gender as a source of joy

Gender as a source of joy

Gender can often feel like a restriction and certainly does have a plethora of negative impacts that progress is slow to fix. However, gender can also be a great source of joy. Playing around with elements of gender expression, finding community, breaking moulds, and feeling confident in your own identity are some of the potential positive impacts.

Part of supporting children's wellbeing is helping build their confidence and self-esteem. Finding joy in aspects of their identity, such as gender, aids this by subverting rigid expectations and limitations typically associated with different identities. This is one of the many ways early years practitioners work to counter discrimination.

Taking an expansive view of gender rather than simply two distinct options helps to open pathways to joy. In accepting gender identity and gender expression as vast, subjective concepts we make space for children to play around and make choices based on what brings them joy as opposed to what is expected of them.

DOI: 10.4324/b23179-3

Gender euphoria

Gender euphoria describes feelings of joy and affirmation when engaging with typically gendered experiences aligning with the individual's identity. Whilst the term "gender euphoria" is typically used by, or about, trans people, that doesn't mean cis people don't experience something similar. It is important to note that the experience may be intensified for trans people as most will have previously had to engage with gendered experiences that felt wrong to them.

Gender euphoria can be based on a range of elements such as physical appearance or expression, correct use of gendered language, or engaging with specific activities. There are no rules to what can and can't make people experience gender euphoria, and there is great variation even within the same gender identities (Beischel et al. 2021).

Gender holds different significance to different people. To some people gender is a totally insignificant part of life, they don't think about it at all or feel that it matters. To others, gender consciously informs their decisions, regarding anything from clothing to friendships and even to jobs. This means people's relationship to gender euphoria will be different. Some people may not experience it at all, and actually an absence of any strong feelings around their gender is the best path to joy.

Children are capable of experiencing gender euphoria in a range of ways. Although young children's understanding of gender tends to be very flexible, development of gender identity is typically thought to happen around age 2, and so engaging with gendered expression has the potential to be a source of joy. The more flexible understanding of gender means that gender euphoria may emerge in unexpected ways through what may seem to be expressions that oppose the child's gender identity.

Supporting children's wellbeing involves noticing, or even just asking, what makes children happy and making opportunities for joy based on those things. There can sometimes be a mentality in continuous provision of "this child always does X thing, let's try not putting it out to make them explore other things". This needs to be adjusted to centre wellbeing, as often what we're really centring by doing this is our own comfort. If a child is always doing the same thing, and it's something that brings them joy, then you should be encouraging that. Gender can absolutely be part of this. It may be that a certain toy or outfit or activity feels affirming to a child, and so by repeating it they gain a sense of self-assurance.

Gender in friendships

As with all facets of identity, there is a joy to be found in engaging with people we can recognise our own experiences in. Gender (and perceived gender) impacts the way we interact with the world and the way others interact with us, and this can create a sense of safety in forming friendships with people who share a lot of aspects of our identities. That being said, there is potential for harm in encouraging this as isolating people from each other reinforces divisions in ways that lead to discrimination.

A well-established idea within early years is encouraging children to get along with each other regardless of differences. In fact, "we're all friends here" is a common phrase to hear in settings. There is a need for balance here where we are allowing children to make choices about who they are friends with whilst encouraging them to get on with a range of people.

Attempted solutions to gender divides in friendships have typically included things like assigning a "boy, girl, boy, girl" seating pattern at lunchtimes. There's nothing wrong with encouraging children to spend time with different people to who they normally play with. However, sometimes if we make this an assignment we can actually be discouraging new friendships instead as children could focus on the fact they've been separated from their friends rather than on talking to someone new.

Children can associate positive traits with their own gender but negative traits with others (Kuhn et al., 1978). It's likely this is a factor in why friendships often have a gender divide, and so fostering positive relationships between children beyond their own experience of gender necessitates promoting empathising with and seeing positive traits in other genders.

Problems can occur when someone of a different gender wants to play with a group who are all the same gender as each other. Whilst there are plenty of children who wouldn't even think twice about this, a variety of factors including the way adults interact, books, TV shows, etc., can lead children to think excluding people based on gender is acceptable. It is possible to use these moments to turn inviting different people to play into a source of joy. Preventing harm has to be the immediate priority and so it's important to lead with something that makes it clear they are allowed to join. There may be situations where not acknowledging gender further is appropriate but sometimes it will be possible to use this as an opportunity to discuss that it is a positive thing when someone different joins in, or that different genders can find joy in the same types of play.

Playing around with new ideas

There is also joy to be found in exploration and experimentation with things outside of our typical identities. Early years should be all about play, and being able to play with things that feel different or even strange can be freeing. For example, a child may like to engage in fancy dress with clothes not typically associated with their gender specifically because it feels fun and silly. As long as we can make sure they aren't responding to other people's exploration in the same way, and of course not telling a child they look silly, it's fine to let children enjoy that feeling of doing something strange to them.

A story from my own practice comes to mind where children playing house were fighting over who could be "mummy" and I reminded them some of their friends had two mummies. One child responded "what about four mummies?" This led to a game with a lot more mums than you'd likely find in a real-life family where all involved were having fun and laughing about it. Obviously, it wouldn't have been okay to encourage them to laugh at the idea of two mummies, and it's certainly possible in families to have more than that. However, allowing the joke of more and more mummies not only diffused the conflict but broke the pattern of the game in a way that led to a lot of fun and creativity in a game that can become quite repetitive.

Representation

Representation is one way we can create joy by utilising gender. Children need to see characters that look like them in resources and books. It can be fun to look together to find characters that look like ourselves or each other. If your resources don't actively reflect the children in your setting then not everyone can feel included.

Beyond just appearance, the representation of characters enjoying different elements of gender expression or typically gendered activities is important too. Beyond looking at books, this is something we can reinforce in how we set up and engage with resources. For example, when engaging with children in small world play if we always use the same dolls following the same patterns which reinforce gender roles that sends a message about real-life expectations. By making sure that we vary how we engage and actively choosing to subvert stereotypes we are creating a positive space for affirming freedom from those expectations.

Gender euphoria in books

A great example of gender euphoria in a book that's perfect for early years settings is *Julian Is a Mermaid* by Jessica Love. It utilises the metaphor of mermaids to represent a trans experience in a beautiful picture book. Julian watches the mermaids and tells his grandma that he wants to be one. She supports him and he uses her clothes and accessories to dress himself as a mermaid. This is a very visually pleasing book which has several pages of wordless illustrations showing Julian's transformation. The limited use of words combined with the stylised, colourful artwork make this an engaging read for young children and something they can enjoy looking at independently. The downside of the use of a mythical creature that's frequently used in children's media and dressing up as a metaphor is that it's possible to disregard the gender euphoria element; because children of all genders can (and do) dress up as mermaids. As early years practitioners we can bring this into discussion around the story, and the book containing so few words does lend itself to a more collaborative, conversational reading time. It's important to get the most out of books heavy on metaphor in conversations about gender, especially when they are a representation of the joy gender can bring.

Dolls

Beyond just examining who your dolls represent, the ways they can be set out and played with are important in utilising them to create joy.

Ideally, have dolls with changeable clothing at least. That way children can play around with different ways to make dolls look more like themselves or people they know, or just play around trying different styles on different dolls.

There are also magnetic or puzzle-type resources that have a body as a base and then elements such as clothes, shoes, hair, and jewellery being separate pieces so that children can play around. This is also something that could be created using magnetic sheets with images glued on top. This would then leave room for expanding the set over time and allowing children's input about what to add. This type of play can be a great way to have conversations about how different elements of expression can feel.

In craft activities that involve creating people, make sure there are a variety of resources and examples, and that these aren't separated into gendered categories. For example, if you were to set up a table to make paper dolls, putting long hair and dresses in one pot and short hair and trousers in another reinforces that those things "belong" together. It's generally best practice to make craft opportunities as open-ended as possible to encourage creativity and active learning.

Gender expression

Gender expression refers to aspects of appearance, such as hair and clothing, that can be feminine, masculine, or androgynous. Feeling that our gender expression correctly identifies our gender to others (or causes deliberate uncertainty) can be a source of joy. Often young children have very limited control over these things and so their gender expression is determined by what their parents or careers provide.

An example of how we can normalise children making choices free from gender restrictions is by rearranging spare clothes into non-gendered categories such as separating tops into long sleeves and short sleeves. When a child needs to change into them show them options based on what might physically fit them, not based on what you think they should wear. Some children may say something like "that's not for girls", if they aren't used to being allowed to choose or given a range of clothing at home. This is an opportunity to explain that anyone can wear anything they want, and that means if they don't want to wear something they are free to express that too.

Allowing staff flexibility in presentation is useful as children will then be forming relationships and spending a lot of time around people who look different. Even though statistically speaking early years staff are quite a narrow demographic, there are factors of expression in hair, clothing, tattoos, and piercings that children can benefit from having normalised.

CASE STUDY – HARRY

Harry, a non-speaking child, went to pick a dress from the dressing-up and bring it over to me. I asked him, "Do you want this on?" He shook his head and pointed to a girl. Although I explained he could wear it if he wanted, he continued to shake his head so we moved on to a different activity. He repeated this process every day for weeks, going to pick out a dress and then pointing at a girl who should wear it. I tried to offer reassurance that he could wear it when he felt ready without putting pressure on him. After several weeks of this, he eventually nodded when I asked if he wanted to wear it. After I put it on him I asked, "Do you like it?" He smiled and nodded. For the rest of his time at my setting, he put on a dress almost every day.

This was a clear example of the way children will have already internalised ideas about what boys and girls are allowed to do. He very obviously wanted to put the dress on but truly believed it wasn't an option for him. By consistently offering reassurance that it was up to him whether to wear it, I was able, over time, to get him to feel comfortable enough to try it out. Partly I believe this was achieved by de-emphasising the role of gender in his decision. Of course, there are many instances where it is useful to affirm that people of certain genders can do things that go against expectations but when talking to an individual it can be more powerful to affirm that they, specifically, are allowed to make their own choices.

REFLECTION POINT

Take some time to think about what brings you joy. Are there certain clothes, hairstyles, or products that make you feel happier than others? For some people, there will be a clear thread of enjoying femininity, androgyny, or masculinity. For others, there may not be a stand-out preference, or engaging with different elements at once may be a source of joy.

Ultimately, what's considered masculine or feminine isn't universal and shifts over time so different people may be drawn to the same item but with opposite perceptions of it. That's why taking the time to reflect on what we enjoy, how we perceive those things, and why we enjoy them is important. It may even lead to realisations that some elements of gender expression we are engaging with are because of expectations rather than because they actually bring us joy.

Knowing what feels good to us and seeking it out is important in protecting our own joy. It can be easy to avoid analysing our own feelings and what may be causing them, and it may even feel silly to acknowledge that a seemingly trivial matter like nail varnish, for example, can impact how we feel about ourselves. Not only do we owe it to ourselves to figure out how to find our own joy, but also when we feel happy and affirmed in our gender we are better able to support children to feel that happiness too. Demonstrating curiosity about children's preferences and being able to express our own helps to normalise seeking affirmation, which will in turn bolster children's confidence.

Brain mosaics

Although the idea of males having masculine traits and females having feminine traits still prevails, research supports the concept that it's far more common to have a mixture of traits than it is to fit neatly into societal expectations of what a man or woman should be.

Joel et al. (2015) referred to this concept as the "human brain mosaic" and concluded that a shift was necessary "from thinking of brains as falling into two classes, one typical of males and the other typical of females". They posited instead we must "appreciate the variability of the human brain mosaic". Our perception, then, of gender as a source of joy must encapsulate this variation.

Enjoyment of femininity and masculinity isn't dependent on assigned gender or even gender identity but rather something everyone has the potential to engage with. The division of masculine and feminine is based on ideas we now know aren't true so perhaps one day those labels won't exist at all in the common lexicon. In our current practice, we must reflect on the role assumptions of two distinct, gender-based brain types have played in the way we interact with and celebrate children. Whilst we've gone over why children may need encouragement to engage with things not typically associated with their gender, it's possible to fall into the trap of then seeing a particular child as a 'feminine boy' or 'masculine girl'. Reimagining gender as a source of joy means seeing every child as a unique individual with their own thoughts, feelings, and preferences without any expectation of a pattern of linked gendered traits.

As well as embedding this concept into our practice and interactions with children, this could make for an interesting activity in settings. Start with an outline of a brain or a person and divide it up into pieces either by drawing lines or cutting them out. Provide different colour paint or pencils, or even different craft materials for sticking, and ask children what they like about themselves, or what makes them happy. Each thing they say becomes a piece of the mosaic; you or the child could write what they say and then they can decorate over it however they want to. When all the pieces are complete put them back together. Children will then have a unique visual representation (however abstract it turns out to be) of sources of joy within themselves. It's also likely some children won't be particularly interested in the conversation aspect and just want to engage in the crafting, which must be respected as its own source of joy!

Protecting joy: talking to families

It's not uncommon for practitioners to come across families who have a very binary understanding of gender and how those genders should behave. This can lead to uncomfortable situations where a parent or carer asks that you stop their child from playing with or wearing particular outfits that deviate from their expectation of what their child should be choosing. Although it is important to take a firm stance against setting limitations in setting, these conversations must be approached from a place of understanding in order to help guide the parent or carer to better understand the importance of letting children play how they choose. If what we can provide for the child is a safe space and time to engage with things they enjoy but wouldn't typically be encouraged to do, that can absolutely have a positive impact. However, if we can help shift the mindset of the family we may open up space for the child to experience that joy at home too.

More often than not, a parent's or carer's negative response to their child playing with something unexpected for their gender comes from a lack of understanding as opposed to a place of malice. Asking more questions for clarity on why they object to their child's choice can help practitioners gauge how to approach the conversation. Sometimes, the beliefs the parent or carer has expressed aren't something they've really examined themselves, and so being asked why they've made a particular comment can spark self-reflection as to whether limiting their child's options based on gender really aligns with their beliefs as well as their hopes for their child's future. A common reason parents or carers may ask for their child not to be allowed to engage with certain things is that they have misconceptions about toy and clothing choices indicating sexuality. It's easy in these circumstances to jump to reassurance that toy and clothing choices children make have nothing to do with sexuality, which is true and worth discussing. However, by focusing on the lack of correlation as a way to placate parents or carers it's possible to end up reinforcing the idea of some sexualities being negative and almost reassuring parents that their child is straight when in reality this shouldn't matter and isn't something we usually know about children.

Advocating for joy

Children may need encouragement to play or wear something different from their usual and there are many ways we can provide this. Whilst many young children make choices about how to engage with resources very freely, others will feel held back by expectations of what they should want to do based on gender.

Modelling enjoyment of a range of activities is one of the most power-ful ways to invite all children in to join you. It's not unusual to have preferences as practitioners on which areas and resources we most enjoy spending time utilising with children. The important thing is that those preferences don't influence children's expectations of the type of person that belongs at each activity. This means getting involved in different areas and inviting children in by showing your own enjoy-ment and encouraging them to try new things with you. You may even find there are things you were discouraged from liking as a child that you actually quite enjoy. None of this means you can't ever express a dislike of something; it can be helpful for children to understand that we all have preferences that should be respected, but we mustn't pass our dislikes on.

Advocating for joy means recognising potential barriers to it. A boy in your setting might have the same desire as a girl in your setting to pretend to be a princess. The difference is that the girl will likely have seen countless people who look like her doing that, whereas the boy could easily have seen none. This means you may need to offer dif-ferent encouragement. You need to anticipate that other children or, unfortunately, staff might laugh or make a comment and be ready to intercept. Several children's films and TV programmes feature the same joke where a man ends up in a dress and is humiliated and it's all hilarious. Awareness of the precious thing that is a child doing what they want despite societal or cultural expectations is essential here and we need to actively advocate for joy in order to nurture this.

Drag story time

"Drag" refers to the performance of exaggerated femininity, mascu-linity, or other forms of gender expression and can be used for per-formance or just for fun. It is a great example of utilising gender as a source of joy, as it allows for playful exploration of gender as a sort of costume. In the UK, children most often first experience drag performance as an integral part of pantomimes.

In recent years, drag performers have been running events for children, usually involving someone in drag reading stories to children at libraries and other venues. These events prioritise fun and encouraging children's imaginations. Drag Queen Story Hour UK say they "want to show the world that being different is not a bad thing", which is a message shared in the aims of a lot of early years guidance. Drag story times have been positively received by those that attend them, and children get the benefits of a fun and unique experience alongside the usual benefits of being read to.

Conclusion

There are many ways in which gender can be utilised as a source of joy when practitioners take an active role in encouraging joy without reinforcing gender roles. Joy is an important aspect of wellbeing alongside being able to experience and express a full spectrum of emotion. Being able to identify and seek out things that make us happy is an important skill to teach children in order for them to continue supporting their own wellbeing. Ultimately, we want early years settings to be a place that's full of joy so that we can maximise the positive impact we have on children's development.

Further learning

Tara M. Chaplin and Amelia Aldao's meta-analysis titled "Gender Differences in Emotion Expression in Children" examines the role of expectations set by gender on the emotions children feel and how they express these emotions.

Jorezza Antonio's blog "Friendships between Kids of Different Genders" (https://www.kidsacademy.mobi/storytime/different-gen-ders-kids-friendship/) explains why friendships with different genders are important, and ways to encourage and support children's friendships.

Laura Kate Dale's book *Gender Euphoria: Stories of Joy from Trans, Non-binary and Intersex Writers* is a collection of writing focused on joyful experiences of gender affirmation.

References

Beischel, W. J., Gauvin, S. E. M., and van Anders, S. M. (2021, May 3) "A little shiny gender breakthrough: Community understandings of gender euphoria". *International Journal of Transgender Health*, 23(3), 274–294. doi:10.1080/26895269.2021.1915223. PMID: 35799953; PMCID: PMC9255216.

Chaplin, T. M., and Aldao, A. (2012, July) "Gender differences in emotion expression in children: A meta-analytic review". *Psychological Bulletin*, 139(4), 735–765. doi: 10.1037/a0030737. Epub 2012 December 10. PMID: 23231534; PMCID: PMC3597769.

Joel, D., Berman, Z., Tavor, I., Wexler, N., Gaber, O., Stein, Y., Shefi, N., Pool, J., Urchs, S., Margulies, D. S., Liem, F., Hänggi, J., Jäncke, L., and Assaf, Y. (2015) "Sex beyond the genitalia: The human brain mosaic". *Proceedings of the National Academy of Sciences*, 112(50), 15468–15473. https://doi.org/10.1073/pnas.1509654112

Kuhn, D., Nash, S. C., and Brucken, L. (1978, June) "Sex role concepts of two- and three-year-olds". *Child Development*, 49(2), 445–451. PMID: 679779.

Love, J. (2018) *Julian Is a Mermaid*. Walker Books.

https://www.dragqueenstoryhour.co.uk

Empowering children in their exploration of identity

Empowering children in their exploration of identity

Early years settings are naturally full of opportunities to utilise imaginative play to explore and support the idea of self-identification. Children learn about themselves and the world around them through experimenting and building a range of experiences to draw conclusions from and develop preferences. "Playing and exploring" is a subheading in the characteristics of effective learning so we must recognise the importance of facilitating experimentation in aiding children's development.

Empowerment is about instilling confidence and strength so that children are able to view themselves positively and practice autonomy. Early years settings are often the first opportunity children have to spend significant amounts of time away from their family, and as such this is often where children are able to access a broader range of opportunity. Continuous provision means children are encouraged to make their own choices and form their own opinions and, as early years practitioners, we need to be prepared to support and encourage this. Empowerment involves making sure no child feels limited by any element of their identity.

Early years settings provide a space separate from children's home life and their families' expectations, and so children begin to explore

DOI: 10.4324/b23179-4

identity independently. A child's role within their family significantly impacts who they are at home, but in early years settings there is freedom from that in allowing children space to experiment with who they are and how they relate to others in a new environment.

All about me folder

It's very common for "all about me" forms to be included as part of admissions as a way for parents and carers to give some basic information that can be used to help children with settling. However, often nothing really happens to them after that initial read-through by the key person other than being stored and maybe glanced at as a refresher.

All about me forms vary from setting to setting but are typically a set of basic questions about the child that their key person will find useful in understanding how to help settle and support them. Preferences, things children need support with, and who the important figures are in a child's life are all part of their individual identity.

The idea of an all about me folder is to compile forms and have them in the setting somewhere children can look at and talk about them. Photographs from home and within the setting can be added to make the forms more visually interesting. Children will enjoy looking through to find themselves and their friends, and this is a great opportunity for children to talk about themselves. Practitioners can read out the answers given by parents and encourage children to give their own answer, and revisit those answers later on. There's no reason these forms can't be seen as on ongoing document that children can alter or add to.

Figure 4.1 A table set up with activities that look at identity including maps, wooden people, diverse books, and an all about me folder.

Dressing up

There is often debate about what dressing up should consist of in early years settings and whether providing familiar, complete costumes is more limiting creatively than having different fabrics. There is value in both things, and sometimes opposing having character costumes comes from an incorrect assumption all children will have access to these at home.

Ultimately there's no right or wrong way to dress up. One child may enjoy dressing up as their favourite character and using that as a base to act out stories. Another child may drape and tie different fabrics around themselves and explain an invented character in great detail. Another child may enjoy putting on a fairy dress and then playing something totally irrelevant, just wearing a fairy dress instead! All three have the opportunity to be empowering in different ways. Dressing as an admired character might provide confidence. Sometimes children are drawn to characters that have character traits or powers they wish they had. Sometimes children are drawn to characters they wish they looked like.

You can help empower children's play when dressing up by asking questions about who they are being and affirming their answers. The more open ended the questions are the better in encouraging children's creativity and allowing freedom for them to make their own choices not influenced by your assumptions. Even though roles created can be very abstract and/or fictional, the acceptance provided by going along with the child's idea helps send the message to children that they get to define who they are and have that respected by those around them.

Making the most out of the home corner

The home corner provides the most direct tie-in to why the play instinct exists at all – to act out a range of situations in a safe way so that we develop the skills to survive ahead of them being needed. It seems a logical next step then to create a space where children feel empowered to explore.

Not everybody's home life looks exactly the same so, even when sticking to simpler home corner set-ups, it's important to honour cultural variation around what home might look like or feel like to different children. Broadening selections of cutlery, toy foods, cooking utensils, and recipe books is one of the ways more children can feel their home is represented. Layout can also be varied as not everyone sits at the table to eat. Some families may use the floor, a table that's low to the ground, or sit on the sofa.

Home corners also don't always have to mimic home. Setting out an airport or a building site, for example, can encourage the exploration of totally different roles. Utilising the example of an airport, props such as passports can be created by children as a way of encouraging the exploration of identity. This could be in the form of getting children to think about themselves and build an accurate image or could take the form of creating a silly character. An airport may be less recognisable both because of setting limitations and the fact not all children will have been to one. This provides an opportunity to really talk through and collectively imagine the location and the different roles available.

Professions

Empowering children's exploration of identity includes helping them to feel that their aspirations don't have to depend on having a specific identity. Feeling that certain aspects of identity restrict our options can get in the way of fully exploring and enjoying that exploration.

Although there has been some level of progress it's undeniable that societal expectations of what jobs people can do based on gender are still around. Some of these limitations are based on outdated ideas of women being nurturers or helpers whilst men are the leaders and breadwinners. It's been assumed these ideas about distinct jobs were always around, starting with men as hunters and women as gatherers. However, a more recent analysis of data from 53 foraging societies around the world revealed that in at least 79% of these societies, women took part in hunting (Anderson, A et al., 2023).

Children shouldn't feel their aspirations are limited based on any facet of their identity.

Imaginative play relating to professionals must be made welcoming to all. Think about the role you take when playing alongside children. It may be that you feel more comfortable joining some roleplays than others but this can mean missing out on opportunities to model or talk about different kinds of people being able to achieve the same things.

If your early years settings have visits relating to professions it's good practice to seek out multiple professionals of different genders and identities who do the same job. By showing children just one example, or multiple examples who all look the same, this sets an expectation of who exactly can enter that profession.

Subconsciously making children feel limited by gender

As Gina Rippon explained in *The Gender Brain: The New Neuroscience That Shatters the Myth of the Female Brain* (2019), "Stereotypes could be straitjacketing our flexible, plastic brains. So, yes, challenging them does matter". Whilst it's unlikely practitioners are trying to enforce stereotypes, it's inevitable that we all have absorbed them and, if we don't take active steps to address and challenge them, will end up perpetuating them in our practice.

I think most early years practitioners will be able to recall a time when a girl was brought in wearing a very pretty, fancy, stainable dress. Sometimes this will even be accompanied by a parent or carer asking the child and/or you to be careful with the dress. This sets a limitation on activity that is rarely (though, of course, not never) placed on boys. Prioritising clothing over play is clearly not aligned with best practice in early years, yet it's very easy to fall into the trap of doing so. Even practitioners who try to find solutions rather than dictate what the child can and can't do may be emphasising the importance of the dress with comments such as "let's put an apron on to keep your pretty dress clean".

Ideally, we can prevent situations like this arising altogether. It's important to set an expectation that clothes will definitely get messy and so nothing important, expensive, or hard to clean is appropriate. This can be done during show-arounds, admission and be in your policies/parent information packs.

We must try to avoid sparking defensiveness by becoming argumentative if it does happen, especially in front of the child, but also try not to agree to keep anything clean if that gets requested at drop off. The best way to manage the conversation will depend on the parent/carer and the dynamic you have with them. Sometimes a "can't promise no mess unfortunately" will be enough, but for others the clothing may feel like an important enough issue to keep pressing. Of course, there's multiple possible reasons the clothing may genuinely be important, for example, cost or sentiment.

Affirming self-identification

Encourage children's exploration by accepting their roleplay and affirming the role they have chosen. It may not seem particularly important to acknowledge that a child is being their favourite character or animal, but refusing to go along with children's pretence sends a message that their play isn't valuable. If a child is using their roleplay to explore possible identities, whether that be related to gender identity or not, then failing to support and affirm this could cause deeper harm wherein a child learns that they will not be listened to or respected when sharing discoveries about themselves.

We all know people who don't go by the name on their birth certificate and there are a number of reasons for this. Gender can play its part here in obvious ways such as someone whose name is almost always given to girls feeling that they need a name that's more common for boys. It can also be gender related in subtler ways such as going by a nickname that's more neutral. It's also not necessarily about statistics surrounding which names "belong to" which gender; after all, the masculinity and femininity of names isn't a fixed or objective judgement.

Educators must respect children's right to self identify. This can take a range of forms as children play around with and develop their own identities. Childcare and educational settings are often the first place children are spending a significant amount of time away from their parents/guardians. This means it's likely to be the children's first opportunity to explore their own opinions, preferences, and feelings outside of their family's influence, and so it's important to remember that educators have a responsibility to encourage that exploration.

When it comes to young children establishing their identity, sometimes encouraging them to express themselves might take the form of serious conversations wherein children are confiding something, or expressing distress about their own identity. Other times this will take the form of a child insisting you call them their favourite character's name all day. Both are essential opportunities to affirm children's right to define their own identity, and to insist that be respected.

 REFLECTION POINT

What makes you feel empowered in your own identity? Children can pick up on how we feel about ourselves, so if we can model empowerment and affirmation this increases our chances of passing this on to them. Make sure to keep engaging with things you find empowering, whether that's activities, words, friendships, etc. It can be easy to let these things slip when we're as stressed and busy as early years practitioners tend to be, but if we lose our own sense of identity to our work then we can't be good role models for empowerment for the children in our care.

CASE STUDY – ELLIE

I was reading the book *Mummy, Mama and Me* to a small group of children. Afterwards, Ellie asked "is that two mummies?" I explained that, yes, the story was about a family with two mummies and that some of our friends at pre-school have two mummies as well. Ellie said "It's okay, it's just different but it's okay".

I've read this book (and *Daddy, Papa and Me*) multiple times. Most of the time there's no comment at all on the family presented in the story, and every so often there's curiosity about it. This particular occasion stands out to me as one of the only times it was clear a child had already had differences in orientation explained. We know that children repeat what they hear and are very receptive to new ideas. This is why it is so important to actively discuss elements of identity such as gender and sexuality and do everything we can to inspire acceptance.

Book recommendation

Perfectly Norman is a part of Tom Percival's "big bright feelings" series, all of which encourage children to examine and talk about their own feelings and where they come from. The story begins with Norman, who had always been "normal", growing wings. This is incredibly exciting to him at first but then he realises they make him stand out as different and so decides he has to hide them. Norman becomes isolated and unhappy; the book guides children to realise that it's not being different that's upsetting, it's feeling like you have to hide a part of yourself. Whilst our bookshelves must contain books about diversity without metaphors, *Perfectly Norman* provides a great starting point for open discussions about differences and is especially a good fit for meaningful conversations about gender, sexuality, and neurodivergence. Even some of our youngest children will already be aware of feeling different, even if they have no idea what that difference will come to mean, and they need to know that they aren't alone. *Perfectly Norman* promotes teaching children early on that diversity is beautiful, and that being open about our differences is a brave and powerful thing to do.

Involving children in observations

An often underutilised opportunity for empowerment is giving children understanding of the observation process and allowing them to input. Many settings use photo observations and this is an ideal opportunity to get children involved in enjoying sharing creations and being confident seeing themselves in photos.

Although broader consent for photos is established by parents, it can be beneficial to try asking children in the moment, "Can we take a picture of this to show your family?" Then you can show children the pictures you've taken to talk over and find out if they like them.

In my own practice I have found that, over time, children will start to take a more active role in observations and some will make requests to take photos or videos of something they're proud of or want their family to see. This is a great way to empower children to feel proud of trying or achieving new things.

This may also mean re-examining how observations are done in your setting. There are lots of differing opinions on this and the same things won't necessarily work for all. In my own practice I've found the method that got most engagement from children and their families was to focus on collecting and putting up a selection of pictures all together with accompanying text being a brief explanation of what was happening in some of them or pointing out a certain achievement.

Figure 4.2 A big piece of green play dough on a blue table with shells around it. The play dough has pattern indents from the shells.

This gives everyone a better sense of what a child enjoys and what's important to them than observation styles that are more focused on tracking for example.

REFLECTION POINT

It's easy for "paperwork" elements of being an early years practitioner to begin to feel purposeless. Think about observations you've done and how you felt about them. Are your observations really achieving anything? A good observation system should be encouraging communication with families, helping you to learn more about the child, and solidifying how best to work with that child's needs and interests.

Promoting good self-esteem

Part of empowering children's exploration of identity is building confidence and a positive self-image. Gender is a factor in self-esteem in that certain images are promoted as to what boys and girls should look like. This can then feel like a standard that has to be achieved and looking different is a failure of that.

It's important to be aware of your own behaviour around children. If you're avoiding looking at your reflection, ducking out of photos, or talking negatively about yourself this could normalise self-deprecation and cause children to feel bad about their own appearance. It's perfectly understandable for people of any age to have complicated feelings about mirrors and photographs, and we're often not exactly looking our best doing a job that can be very active and get very messy.

There is a marked difference in how people respond to girls using "boys'" toys and clothing and how people respond to boys using "girls'" toys and clothing. Femininity is often seen as shameful in a way that masculinity isn't. Overcoming that shame for people of all genders is necessary for improving wellbeing. That's not to say girls engaging with masculinity never face backlash for that, but the focus on shame differs.

Shame is a huge barrier to empowerment as it negatively impacts confidence. If children feel ashamed to explore or express preferences for certain things then they are not able to truly engage with exploring their identity.

PRACTITIONER REFLECTION – KERRY MURPHY

As educators, we have a significant role in shaping children's personal and social identities. We do this by observing, assessing, and planning for their development, implementing curriculums and frameworks, and adopting child-centred pedagogies. These activities are generally considered good and well intentioned, and to a large extent they are. However, in recent years, I have become cautious about how we convey to children, both directly and indirectly through these activities, that there is a "right" or expected way of being. Unfortunately, this often translates into reinforcing heteronormative and neuronormative standards and can also lead us to de-centre children's autonomy in shaping their own identities.

For example, from a heteronormative perspective, we might reinforce gender stereotypes by encouraging children to play with particular toys or project gender schema onto our environment, which promotes binary thinking, such as spaces for boys and spaces for girls. We might go one step further and actively discourage children from exploring beyond our limited gendered expectations.

From a neuronormative perspective, we might expect all children to meet milestones on similar timelines, or we may judge certain children's play as weird if it does not conform to social expectations. For example, we might judge an autistic child for hand flapping excitedly during play or for getting sensory highs from repeating the same play patterns.

Both heteronormativity and neuronormativity are upheld by a need for compliance and conformity to socially constructed ideas of normalcy. However, in my years of caring for and educating young children, I have noticed that they are not "normal" in the traditional sense, and this is actually a positive thing. Children are weird in the best ways because they show us how to resist and subvert normalcy. Who they are in their earliest years is not predetermined, and their very existence demonstrates something called neuroqueerness. Dr Nick Walker has coined the term "neuroqueering", which refers to the practice of queering (subverting, defying, disrupting, and liberating oneself from) neuronormativity and heteronormativity simultaneously (2021).

I often hear young children being referred to as "unruly", "disobedient", or poorly behaved, but I have come to realise that, in many ways, they are simply embodying their neuroqueer selves. They have not yet succumbed to the neuronormative and heteronormative world imposed upon them. As educators, we have a responsibility to provide children with play-filled, loving, safe, and joyful lives. But we must also recognise that the ways in which we are expected to facilitate this can also be driven by frameworks that train children out of their neuroqueer selves. So, how might we embrace neuroqueering in an early childhood space? Much of Walker's work explores how conditioned adults might undo some of this to rediscover their neuroqueering ways. However, with children, we can assume it as their natural ways of being. To be curious rather than concerned about their play, learning, and development is a good starting point. For example, rather than normalise or "neurostraighten" their play patterns, we join in, mirror, and embrace even that which doesn't make sense to us. We can also move away from standardisation practices such as having prescribed social rules or "one size fits all" expectations, for example, demanding eye contact during interactions, or expecting certain behaviours from a child based on their assumed gender.

Finally, we should take time to learn about the ways in which we have been conditioned by neuronormativity and heteronormativity and interrogate how much of this actually contributes to our own wellbeing, joy, and sense of belonging.

Open discussions about gender

We have to be aware that there are people who hold very outdated, overly simplistic, harmful beliefs about gender and that children will encounter these views at some point. This is why we have to be pro-active in teaching children acceptance and empathy so that when those ideas are heard children are able to recognise them as wrong. If the first voices children hear discussing gender inclusion are speaking negatively then they are much more likely to believe it than if they've already learned about those concepts.

The idea open conversations about gender, or any aspect of diversity for that matter, are too difficult to navigate only serves to uphold oppressive systems by creating a culture that discourages open dialogue about discrimination, reinforcing a wilful lack of awareness from oppressive groups. This means that in the early years, we have the opportunity to normalise open conversation and begin to break this cycle. Engaging children in such conversation isn't necessarily a process of engineering dialogue. Children will talk about their differences and will share their observations about the world much more freely than adults, so facilitating these discussions is a primary way we encourage open discussions about diversity. By failing to take these opportunities as they arise in favour of brushing over anything we feel discomfort talking about we create the idea of some topics being forbidden. Instead, we must take the opportunity provided to open a dialogue about gender that shows their curiosity is valued.

The concept of gender transformative education, put forward in a publication supported by Plan International, Transform Education, UNGEI, and UNICEF, is to move beyond the idea of improving opportunities for marginalised genders to focus on actively challenging the norms and power imbalances causing inequality of opportunity. As laid out in the aims for reimagining education, "imagine if every child and young person had the tools, knowledge and resources to challenge the status quo and champion gender equality from a young age" (Gender Transformative Education, 2021). This work requires a multi-sectoral approach but ultimately centres on educational settings as a place of significant influence on children's understanding of existing norms and how to challenge them, and it is emphasised this must begin in early childhood education.

Empowering children's exploration of identity means giving them the tools necessary to recognise and dismantle oppressive rhetoric surrounding gender. This includes using books, resources, your own stories, and organic opportunities to talk about what gender is and why attempts to create division based on gender are wrong. Even acknowledging that gender is expansive and not just about two types of people based on two over-simplified categorisations of bodies is a positive first step.

We need to encourage children's inquisitive natures and that will sometimes mean dealing with questions we aren't sure we can answer. You can learn together with children by researching alongside them using technology (with prior consideration of safety settings) and by sharing ideas and asking questions in return. You are allowed to admit that you don't know the answer. In fact, doing so empowers children by teaching them that being curious and seeking knowledge is more important than having all the answers. In such a busy environment it's understandable to want or need to brush things off, but the potential negative impact this could have means even if you have to tell children you'll revisit a conversation later (and actually follow this through) it is worth it.

REFLECTION POINT

Power dynamics in any educational setting can be complicated, especially so with very young children who have such limited independence. Practitioners are, of course, in control of the setting overall. However, being in a position of power doesn't mean exerting control for no reason. It's easy to fall into the habit of giving instructions or enforcing rules that don't necessarily have solid reasoning behind them.

Can you think of a time a child questioned why you were telling them to do (or stop doing) something? Did you explain it or just attempt to establish your authority as reason enough? Instructions we give or demands we make should be explainable beyond "because I said so". It may feel frustrating to have children that push back on authority but the best way to avoid this problem is through cultivating mutual respect and trust.

Figure 4.3 A practitioner and a child sat next to each other playing the drums. The practitioner is watching the child and following what she does.

Conclusion

Exploration of identity is an essential, lifelong process that we must strive to maximise opportunity for in our settings in order to build strong foundations for confidence and maintaining flexibility of thinking. We as practitioners play an essential role in both providing opportunity for exploration and actively encouraging children to take those opportunities. We must advocate for children's right to be themselves without feeling boxed in by expectations.

 **Further learning**

Natalie Canning's book *Children's Empowerment in Play: Participation, Voice and Ownership* lays out what it means for children to have empowering experiences, and the overall positive impact they have.

Nick Walker's book *Neuroqueer Heresies: Notes on the Neurodiversity Paradigm, Autistic Empowerment, and Postnormal Possibilities* is a collection of writing around the topic of neuroqueer theory.

References

Anderson, A., Chilczuk, S., Nelson, K., Ruther, R., and Wall-Scheffler, C. (2023) "The myth of man the hunter: Women's contribution to the hunt across ethnographic contexts". *PLoS One,* 18(6), e0287101. https://doi.org/10.1371/journal. pone.0287101

Rippon, G. (2019) *The Gender Brain: The New Neuroscience That Shatters The Myth of the Female Brain.* London: The Bodley Head

UNICEF "Gender transformative education" December 2021 ISBN: 978-92-806-5320-5   https://www.unicef.org/reports/gender -transformative-education

Walker, N (2021) *Neuroqueer Heresies: Notes on the Neurodiversity Paradigm, Autistic Empowerment, and Postnormal Possibilities.* Autonomous Press.

5 | Gendered language

Gendered language

There are many ways in which gender stereotypes are reinforced, one of which is in the language we use. Gendered language is present in our everyday conversations and all around our early years settings to the point it can be difficult to even identify just how much of our language is gendered.

The way adults talk to children can differ based on their own gender and the child's gender (Leaper et al., 1998). It's important to be mindful of this as practitioners as we are modelling language, so if we allow the gender of a child to affect the way we talk to them we risk not fostering the same positive communication development across different genders.

Regardless of intent, gendered language which is exclusionary or discriminatory can cause both immediate and long-term harm for a variety of reasons. Reflecting on how we use gendered language, considering its potential impact, and adjusting our language in response is an important step to take in best supporting children's wellbeing.

DOI: 10.4324/b23179-5

Nursery rhymes

Most early years settings will have a mix of older and newer nursery rhymes in circulation. Singing time can be a great time to bring everyone who wants to participate together in a way that engages children and lets them move and make noise. It's therefore important to examine the content of what we're singing and what messages we might be sending.

I've found that sometimes giving children control of their singing time is the best workaround for stereotypes. For example, when singing "The Wheels on the Bus", asking children to fill in "what's happening on the bus" without offering any prompts usually results in a much more interesting bus that a variety of creatures are on together. This helps us to circumvent the classic lines that perpetuate gender stereotypes whilst also inviting children to lead and create something fun together rather than singing all the same songs the exact same way every day.

It's important not to be scared to scrap songs altogether! There are so many nursery rhymes out there, children aren't going to mourn the loss of one that you feel is outdated, or even just a bit boring. Most children get excited by new songs, especially if they are funny or have a lot of actions to copy. It's possible you'll have disagreements with colleagues about what to scrap, so this may be harder to achieve for some than others. Try to actively work on introducing replacements and make sure you can back up why you want to phase out some of the older ones. The extra effort going into striving for more inclusive practice should be appreciated by colleagues.

Fairy tales

It's important to remember that the fairy tales we tell now have often already strayed from their roots. This means that it's entirely possible to maintain the very important human tradition of passing down stories whilst recognising that as society changes these stories can, and should, change too.

It's also possible to tell a traditional fairy story and discuss issues within it, or why things should be different in real life. For example, we know a common issue with princess stories is that they involve a girl waiting around for a boy to save her.

There are a number of existing retellings of classic fairy tales which seek to diverge from gendered issues prevalent in their original forms. In my own practice I have used two versions of *The New Goldilocks and the Three Bears* by Beth McMurray (2012),one with Daddy and Papa Bear, the other with Mummy and Mama Bear. For children already familiar with the story, understanding that there are multiple ways this story can be told that aren't dependent on gender has the benefit of presenting different families as totally equal. It also presents an opportunity to sidestep gendered and heteronormative stereotypes often present in the story. In my own experience the only time a child ever pointed out that these books strayed from the original story was when a child gasped and said, "It's supposed to be porridge, not soup!"

Much like with scrapping songs, it's important not to be afraid to give away or recycle a book that feels at odds with the setting's ethos, or even just to make way for something different. If you're bored of reading a certain book or you're finding yourself feeling awkward or uncomfortable because it seems a bit outdated or stereotypical then you aren't going to be able to maximise the opportunity for connection and learning that reading to children provides.

REFLECTION POINT

How do you feel about singing and story times in your own practice? It's easy for these activities to become routine fillers, used more as a means of corralling children than as something to really be enjoyed. If it feels as though that's become the case, consider how you might refocus on using rhymes and stories more purposefully. This may mean looking more into how these benefit child development, but should also mean remembering that children are supposed to be having fun in early years settings.

CASE STUDY – TARIQ

I was reading "Sleeping Beauty" to Tariq and could see he was starting to lose focus once we reached the part where Aurora was asleep. I asked, "Do you know this story already?" He said that he did so I asked, "Can you tell me the story instead?" He said, "Well a monster came and it roared really loud to wake her up". I asked if it scared her and he said "No, the monster is her friend". I asked, "What happened after that?" He said, "That's it. He just roared and then they went on an adventure".

This wasn't a retelling that was manufactured on my part but rather an organic opportunity to encourage a child to make their own stories. Sometimes, attachment to traditional stories gets in the way of maximising the value of our interactions with children. I heard many more alternative fairy tales from this particular child by always taking the opportunity to ask whether he wanted to tell me the story instead.

Gendered praise

In repeating the same generic praise are we missing out on opportunities to engage more meaningfully? Tying praise to gender can reinforce stereotypes. The things we praise boys and girls for often differ, and the adjectives we use can feed into outdated ideas about which positive traits belong to which gender.

There are differing opinions on the value of praise for children in general and whether it can interrupt children's ability to follow through on their own ideas and be proud of them in favour of acting in ways they know will elicit praise. Alfie Kohn (2001) argued that praise can actually reduce achievement by presenting success as something easily measured and commented on which can make children feel pressured to replicate that success rather than enjoying the process.

Issues with gendered praise in particular extends to complimenting things children wear or own. If we tell girls how "pretty" their clothing looks and boys how "cool" theirs looks we are subconsciously enforcing a divide in how children should aim to be perceived, as well as potentially connecting this perception of appearance to general likeability. In *The Gender Agenda*, Ros Ball and James Millar noted a time their daughter wanted to wear her bridesmaid dress when visitors were coming and her reasoning was so the visitors "will like (her)". They observed that unfortunately she was right as "A girl in a frilly dress gets a lot of 'Don't you look lovely in your pretty dress!', etc. She obviously associates people appreciating her appearance with being liked."

CASE STUDY – LILY

I was sat with Lily at a table with some paper and pens and I asked if she wanted to draw. She drew a circle with pointy ears and a face and said "Look, it's you!" Earlier in my career I likely would have responded to this with generic praise, but this time I asked, "Is that what I look like?" Lily giggled and started adding lines so I asked, "What are those?" She said, "That's all your legs!" I asked, "How many is that?!" She continued laughing and then got another piece of paper. She continued drawing different versions of me with varying shapes, limbs, and accessories, laughing and adding things when I asked questions.

Sometimes reaching for praise means we miss an opportunity to extend something. Lily did a lot of drawings and showed high levels of engagement throughout, and actively enjoyed my confused responses. Lily showed off her work proudly and laughed when other people confirmed it looked just like me.

Here is my favourite portrait Lily provided of me "as a square, with George's dinosaur and lots of trees".

Figure 5.1 A colourful drawing on white paper of a square person with lots of lines and scribble around.

Gendered nicknames

Early years practitioners will have different ways of addressing children either individually or as a group. Affectionate names like "sweetheart" or "buddy" can often be heard around settings and aren't inherently negative. The issue is when these kinds of words are being used either mostly or entirely towards children of a particular gender.

The line between gendered and not isn't always clear or unchangeable. For example, many people use "guys" as a neutral collective address now to the point where most people won't even notice it as being out of place.

REFLECTION POINT

As well as the broader concept of gendered language it's also important to consider the way we refer to individuals. The most common point of discussion here currently is pronouns, but these aren't the only terms to consider when we think about using language to affirm people's identity. Regardless of whether someone is cisgender or transgender, it's likely there will be some gendered terms that feel good to them, some that feel neutral, and some that feel wrong. Consider reflecting on how you like people to refer to you. This tool is a non-exhaustive list of gendered terms used about an individual with a guide as to how to categorise how you feel about them. This isn't about suggesting everybody should have something like this to hand or should memorise each other's but rather about reflecting on your own feelings, sharing those with whoever you want to, and taking the time to process if others want to share their thoughts with you. There's a tendency to let ourselves feel needless discomfort when it's actually perfectly fine to ask someone to adjust their language and it's important to be receptive when other people ask that of you too. There can be anxiety around making mistakes when using gendered terms but what matters is that you are listening to corrections and trying to get it right.

Figure 5.2 A form laying out different gender terms with boxes and a colour key to fill in indicating preference.

The language surrounding gender identity

As with all elements of identity, community preference on which language feels most appropriate shifts and changes over time. It's important to pay attention to these shifts and to be able to take on corrections without jumping to defensiveness. The terms we use surrounding gender have expanded to provide language for identities that have existed for a long time.

Babies are assigned a sex, male or female, at birth based only on external genitalia. This is significant in that components such as chromosomes are not tested, and there is still no legal recognition of intersex babies who are born with a reproductive or sexual anatomy that doesn't seem to fit the typical definitions of female or male. Therefore, it is considered more accurate to say "assigned female at birth/AFAB" and "assigned male at birth/AMAB'. Cisgender people identify as their assigned gender whereas transgender people do not. The terms "trans" and "non-binary" encompass a broad spectrum of people who don't identify with their assigned gender and this can present in a variety of ways. This all means that we need to respect the name, pronouns, and labels people use, and accept that it isn't our right to question the validity of any of those things. Different people have varying levels of awareness of their own gender identity at different ages and so, even working in early years, we must be willing to prioritise self-identification.

The attainment gap

Statistics often show girls being "ahead" of boys academically in the early years. This starts a pattern that continues in English but splits off in mathematics where boys overtake. This gap isn't biological and certainly shouldn't be accepted as inevitable but rather recognised as a result of socialisation and bias in education.

Whilst there have been a great many studies that claim to have found a biological difference in "male" and "female" brains which explains gendered differences in ability, they are consistently later disproved. For example, a small 1995 study found language-processing to be more evenly spread across hemispheres in women's brains (Shaywitz et al., 1995). A large 2008 meta-analysis then completely disproved these findings (Sommer et al., 2008).

There is a common belief that girls mature faster than boys, but with evidence suggesting there's no such thing as gendered brains this cannot be an innate difference. It's essential then to examine the societal factors which cause this and our role as early years practitioners. We have vastly different expectations of boys and girls in education, which feeds into the attainment gap, thus feeding back into the misconception that girls mature faster. We must reflect on our own expectations of children in our care and whether gender plays a role in that. It's likely we expect certain behaviours based on gender and so respond differently to these expectations being met or unmet.

I remember a conversation I had with a reception teacher who had a majority of boys in their cohort for the first time. She told me she was having to rethink her usual lesson plans to make things "more fun". I wasn't sure what to say at the time but it struck me as such an odd thing to say. Why wouldn't classes that had an equal split or even classes that had more girls than boys want fun? Surely if there are ways you can make your teaching more engaging and enjoyable for the children then that should be what you're doing.

Projecting adult gender and sexuality

Children repeat what they hear so it's important educators understand that having these conversations with children is a part of communicating effectively with parents and carers. Educators will only see parents and carers briefly most of the time, whereas they spend several hours with children so it makes sense to value talking to children about diversity, discrimination, and inclusion as a way of bringing these topics into conversations children will have at home. There will always be a range of parents and carers from those who support introducing these topics to children to those who have outdated views and believe children shouldn't be learning about discrimination. It's therefore important to be prepared to justify why you've had certain conversations with children, and how those conversations were presented to be age-appropriate. In particular, there is a recurring argument that children shouldn't learn about LGBTQ+ identities, stemming from stereotypes of LGBTQ+ people as predatory. Educators must understand the importance of teaching children about different identities, and recognise that children in their care will belong to a range of communities, as well as have clear plans in place to address any backlash.

Children will also repeat what they've heard at home which may sometimes provide insight into where parents or carers stand on particular issues. Occasionally, this might necessitate an uncomfortable conversation if a child has repeated something concerning. It's important to have these conversations and to use them as a learning opportunity for all involved, as leaving bias unquestioned will only reinforce it. If educators approach the conversation with an accusatory tone they are likely to be met with a defensiveness that will shut the dialogue down so it's best to be prepared to give ideas on how they can positively influence the child's views instead of trying to find out where the child's statement came from. Children may also repeat something positive, so it's important educators also recognise that they may learn good ways to talk about diversity and inclusion, or good resources to use, from parents and carers. This can be encouraged further by inviting families to bring books and objects from home, so that they have the opportunity to share elements of what matters to them. Often diverse resources can become tokenistic by treating culture as a costume or reaching for stereotypes so it can be much more productive to utilise resources and stories shared by children and their families.

Family days

Many early years settings have special days when children's parents are allowed to come in with their child. Often the way these have been framed is by having a day for mums and a day for dads. This is not inclusive language as it promotes the idea that all children have a dad and a mum. It is also exclusionary in failing to take into account that not every child will have a parent able to attend.

By reframing these events as "family days" we can extend a more welcoming, inclusive invitation that more children will be able to benefit from.

One example of how invitations to these days may be worded is provided here:

Dear parents/carers

We will be having a family day on (date) and would like to invite one adult per family to join us at (setting) for the day.

We will be having another family day later in the year and encourage a different adult to come to each one if possible as it is a great opportunity for you to see our provision.

We recognise our children have a range of family circumstances, and that not everyone is able to take time off to attend these events. In light of this we will not be restricting which family member or friend known to the child attends but ask that you provide the name of who to expect ahead of time.

Making assumptions about a child's home life

Another way in which we subconsciously reinforce gender bias is when we assume at home there is a traditional family structure, i.e. mummy doing the housework and childcare, daddy going to work and fixing things. An example may be asking a child "What did mummy make you for lunch?" Instead, we can ask "Who made your lunch today? What do you think they put in it?"

Another common time for non-inclusive language is at home time saying "It's time for your mummies and daddies to come", or even "Let's see whose mummy gets here first". It's highly unlikely every child will be being picked up by their mum, and adding dad doesn't really cover all the options either. We see lots of grandparents, friends, and childminders, etc., drop children off and pick them up, so it makes no sense to be exclusionary in the language we use. Personally, I took to replacing saying "your mummies and daddies" with saying "your grown-ups", as this encompasses a broader range of possibilities and as such isn't sending messages about whose job should be whose.

Dividing boys and girls

There are various reasons we may casually group children and often gender is seen as a neat way to do this with a relatively even split. For example, maintaining control during a transitional part of the day like getting ready to go home can be easier if we aren't trying to split attention between all children at the same time. However, gender is far from the only way to do this and utilising it so casually as a divider may be sending negative messages overemphasising the role gender should play and possibly impacting friendships.

In my own practice with an external music company, there is a song that has a section where girls and boys are invited to do actions separately. Whilst this is already an unnecessary thing to include, some practitioners would correct children if they joined in with the "wrong" group. This has the potential to cause harm to children who may already be aware they don't align with their assigned gender or beginning to experience discomfort around gendered terms. It's also a somewhat confusing thing to do; children wanting to join in with songs' actions is a positive thing and so setting rules around when they are and aren't allowed to join in is unnecessarily risking making them less likely to engage in the future.

Other unnecessary divisions could be asking children to line up "girls first" or "boys first". Sometimes making these divisions can help make organising children a smoother process, but utilising gender to do so can send negative messages and encourage gender separation in friendships. Alternative categories can be used and varied each time so that importance isn't assigned to those factors. For example, using age or clothing patterns or favourite food can be more playful ways to form groups. It's also possible to just list children's names and this can be a good way to make sure children are more actively engaged.

Fear of mistakes

It's always better to be actively trying to be as inclusive as possible with your language and make mistakes than it is to never try. As our awareness of the harm certain uses of gendered language can cause increases, it's easy to feel out of the loop. Sometimes our social circles become narrow to the point of almost exclusively talking to people who share our identifiers. Whilst it's understandable to be drawn to people you have easy points of relation to, this isn't conducive to keeping an up-to-date knowledge of language preferences or new points of progress or oppression happening to communities you aren't a part of. Social media means there is a greater accessibility of hearing from a range of people, so although actively trying to meet and engage with a broader range of people can take time, seeking out different voices you aren't hearing from in your day to day is easier than ever.

The other side to this issue is that when you hear people use outdated language it's easy to assume harmful intent or wilful ignorance. As early years practitioners it is important to hold each other accountable in a way that prioritises moving forward together over dividing. Harmful use of gendered language mustn't go ignored, especially in contexts where children or families may have overheard. Sometimes offering a counter example can be beneficial. For example if a colleague says that a child is being a "typical boy" it's usually fairly easy to point out a child of a different gender who engages in the same behaviour, or a child of the same gender that doesn't engage in that same behaviour.

Defaulting to "he"

There is a tendency to always use "he" when talking about animals or objects in play. This can be the case even when looking at a "visibly female" animal toy. It's a common issue and extends to authors as well. This risks contributing to the idea boys are somehow more important or fun as well as creating a lack of visibility for girls and non-binary people.

Varying pronouns when assigning them to characters or toys by making an active choice to use she or they helps normalise different genders as being of equal importance. It's possible when using different pronouns to fall into pairing characters off into pairs of one boy and one girl which can also end up reinforcing ideas about what a normal "couple" is. This means that it's also important to consider how to avoid setting up the same patterns of gender in play to minimise the possibility of replicating expectations of gender roles.

Forms and letters

With most forms and letters being sent home predominantly using the second person and being the same template for all children, a lot of settings won't typically be using gendered language in these instances, particularly for addressing the recipient. However, there are still forms which use phrases like "your son/daughter" when a more inclusive phrasing like "your child" is still correct without being exclusionary. This isn't about eradicating gendered words or dismissing particular genders but rather about making sure everyone feels included.

It's perfectly fine for people to refer to a child being someone's son or daughter when that is the correct word for an individual but when speaking collectively the division is unnecessary and risks excluding some individuals. Use of language in forms and letters can also be a signal of the settings values. If your ethos is said to be one of inclusion but you're handing out letters with unnecessary gendered language this can call into question whether the values you promote are truly being upheld.

Gendered job titles

Utilising gendered job titles can prove to be a difficult habit to break for those of us that were raised with that as the norm. Although it takes a conscious effort, that effort will ultimately help to ease gendered job titles out of the common vernacular in favour of neutral terms.

We know that gender shouldn't dictate which jobs people can or can't do, and we know that we have to encourage children to believe this too. As such, it can be confusing when we are trying to send a message that anyone can achieve anything but then say "fireman" whenever firefighters are brought up. Language matters and the way we use it has to be examined.

There are also instances where the neutral term isn't as well known or there isn't necessarily a unanimously agreed term. "Postman" is a good example here. "Postwoman" has also been in use, albeit less common, for a long time. "Letter carrier" is an older name for the job, whilst now neutral options are more likely to be "postperson" or just "postie".

Conclusion

The relationship between language and gender is complex and deeply embedded, which makes it difficult to examine and unlearn the potentially harmful ways in which we utilise gendered language. Noticing instances of gendered language becomes easier over time when we are consistent in holding ourselves and others accountable and practise making changes as and when we identify our language use as a potential problem. Knowing the real-world negative impact gendered language can have, it is important that we do take those steps in order to provide the best possible care and education for all children in our settings.

Further learning

Marianne Grabrucker documented experiences wherein people perpetuated gender stereotypes to or about her daughter in her book *There's a Good Girl: Gender Stereotyping in the First Three Years of Life: A Diary"*, first published in 1985.

Ros Ball and James Millar decided to write a book with the same concept as Grabrucker's in 2017, titled *The Gender Agenda*.

Josie Cox's article "Language Bias with Kids Entrenches Gender Gaps, Global Study Finds" presents evidence gendered language puts limitations on children's abilities and prospects. https://www.forbes.com/sites/josiecox/2024/03/05/language-bias-with-kids-entrenches-gender-gaps-global-study-finds/

Poetry Basket (https://helicopterstories.co.uk/courses/poetry-basket-1-seasons/) offers sets of videos and downloadable sheets with new nursery rhymes around different themes.

References

Kohn, A. (2001) "Five reasons to stop saying 'good job!'". https://www.alfiekohn.org/article/five-reasons-stop-saying-good-job/

Leaper, C., Anderson, K. J., and Sanders, P. (1998) "Moderators of gender effects on parents' talk to their children: A meta-analysis". *Developmental Psychology*, 34(1), 3–27. https://doi.org/10.1037/0012-1649.34.1.3

McMurray, B (2012) "The new goldilocks and the three bears" CreateSpace Independent Publishing Platform.

Shaywitz, B., Shaywltz, S., Pugh, K., et al. (1995) "Sex differences in the functional organization of the brain for language". *Nature*, 373, 607–609. https://doi.org/10.1038/373607a0

Sommer, I. E., Aleman, A., Somers, M., Boks, M. P., and Kahn, R. S. (2008) "Sex differences in handedness, asymmetry of the Planum Temporale and functional language lateralization." *Brain Research*, 1206, 76–88. ISSN 0006-8993. https://doi.org/10.1016/j.brainres.2008.01.003

6 | Trans and non-binary childhoods

Trans and non-binary childhoods

There is no minimum or maximum age at which trans and non-binary people become aware of their identity but it is clear that gender dysphoria can, and often does, start in the early years. Zaliznyak et al. (2020) found that amongst trans adults seeking gender-affirming care, the majority has memories of experiencing gender dysphoria between ages 4 and 6.

It's understandable to want to shield children from concepts that feel complicated, and it can be upsetting to imagine young children experiencing distress surrounding gender identity. However, through understanding and affirming children's identities, and continuing to strive for a world in which trans and non-binary people are able to live safely and openly as themselves, we can be a part of alleviating that pain.

What is meant by "trans and non-binary childhoods"?

It's true that, in the early years, we won't often come across children who are "out" as trans or non-binary so, whilst it's essential for guidance on how to handle that scenario to exist, practitioners mustn't

DOI: 10.4324/b23179-6

assume that they will always know when a trans or non-binary individual is in their setting. In the vast majority of cases, trans and non-binary people feel that they have always belonged to that identity, regardless of at which point in their life they came to understand that. This means that, even if it wasn't known to themselves or the people around them, they still ultimately experienced a trans/non-binary childhood and deserve to have early years professionals capable of understanding and cultivating a safe, affirming environment.

Gender dysphoria

Gender dysphoria is a strong sense of discomfort with social or physical elements which are typically associated with a particular gender. Physical dysphoria can refer to aspects of appearance or bodily function, whereas social dysphoria has more to do with gendered terms or outward expression. Gender-affirming care refers to anything that helps someone feel more comfortable in their gender identity, for example, changing name and/or pronouns, haircuts, and hormone therapies.

Physical dysphoria is likely to be less obvious until a child becomes aware they are approaching or beginning puberty which will change their body in ways that feel incorrect to them. This is why puberty blockers may be prescribed to children beginning/approaching puberty in order to provide extra time before a decision needs to be made about whether to pursue hormone replacement therapy (HRT), though this is not something that happens within the age range of early years.

Prior to puberty, however, physical differences are much less obvious, and children's understanding of different body types is more limited. This is why physical dysphoria is possible in childhood but may not be the same as physical dysphoria later in life.

Social transition

The idea of children "transitioning" is often brought up as a scare tactic to encourage transphobia. It's important to clarify that "transition" for young children is not about medical intervention, it is a purely social transition. Elements of social transition may include name changes, using different pronouns, and adjusting aspects of gender expression such as clothing and hair in a way that affirms the child's gender identity. No aspect of social transition is irreversible. The way someone feels about themself aged 3 is certainly going to differ from how they feel about themself as an adult, but allowing children the freedom to make decisions about how they look and how they are referred to is important in supporting their wellbeing.

Social transition won't look the same for everyone, as being trans or questioning your gender identity doesn't always mean wanting to fully fit into one of the two pre-existing, distinct gender stereotypes that we know to be reductive. We know that hair length, for example, isn't always indicative of gender amongst cisgender people, so we shouldn't expect everyone wanting to socially transition to view changing their hair as gender affirming.

Early social transition has been consistently found to positively impact children's happiness and overall wellbeing (Horton, 2023). It is therefore essential that we advocate for this should a child in our care express that that is what they want to do.

Retransition

One reason some adults object to supporting children to transition is that they worry children may later change their minds about how they identify. Amongst 317 transgender children, only 7.3% altered their gender identification during a 5-year period, and only 2.5% identified as cisgender after the 5 years according to researchers led by Kristina Olson, PhD, of Princeton University in New Jersey. No aspect of transition that would be undertaken in early childhood is at all irreversible, and so to use the possibility of a child retransitioning as a reason to ignore children's desire to transition is inappropriate.

Jack Turban, MD, MHS, of Stanford University in California, emphasised in an email to MedPage Today that "social transition has value regardless of the ultimate gender trajectory", and that "prohibiting a social transition can send the message to a child that their identity is wrong or invalid, and this can drive shame and damage relationships within a family". It's important to de-emphasise the necessity of certainty that social changes will continue to align with someone's gender identity throughout their life. People grow and change and understanding of our own gender identity can be an element of that.

"Attempts to force transgender children to be cisgender are associated with suicide attempts", he underscored.

CASE STUDY – LEENA

Leena was approaching different members of staff and asking them, "Are you a boy or a girl?" When she asked me I said, "I don't know." She replied, "You don't know?" I asked, "Well what do you think I am?" She looked deep in thought for several seconds and then said, "You look like a girl but you sound like a boy." "Maybe it's both then?" She replied, "Maybe yes", and then went to go and play outside.

I don't necessarily know what she meant by what she said, or if that's how people generally view me. The part of this exchange I value was her receptiveness to questioning. I've often found in conversations with children that they don't particularly know what a boy or girl is and may think it has something to do with names or hair or even favourite colours. This means children often have an easier time than adults accepting gender as an expansive and flexible concept.

Biology

One reason some people struggle to let go of binary gender systems is having been taught that there are two biological sexes and that everyone is one or the other, and it is that biology that determines how someone should present their gender. This isn't true. There's no singular way to define sex, and there are more than two possible sets of chromosomes and variations in factors such as hormone levels which impact physical differences (Fausto-sterling, 1993; Blackless et al., 2000). Many of us actually don't know if our own chromosomes and hormones accurately fit everything assumed from the M or F on our birth certificates.

There is a lot of stigma attached to being intersex, to the extent that parents can be encouraged by doctors to consent for the baby to be operated on, often citing disproved cancer risk. The lack of legal recognition for intersex people means male or female will still be used for legal purposes, and that will usually dictate the gender they are raised as. This also means it's likely you won't know when a child in your setting is intersex. In many ways this highlights the pointlessness of a strictly binary gender social system, as even when we assume physical characteristics dictate gender we know there are people born not fitting neatly into either who are assigned one and raised as such anyway.

Dr Milton Diamond, who was a vocal advocate for intersex people, said ""Nature loves variety, unfortunately society hates it" (2014). It's significant to consider in our roles as early years practitioners that diversity is supposed to exist. The biases we have and the pressures of conformity we risk passing on to children aren't grounded in the reality of nature. We may have been taught rigid rules around biology and identity and it can be difficult to unlearn that, but we can choose not to teach future generations those same things in favour of raising children who understand the importance of accepting and celebrating difference.

Book recommendation

When Aidan Became a Brother by Kyle Lukoff is a book about a trans boy realising his identity and making a social transition. As he awaits the arrival of his younger sibling, Aidan becomes anxious that his parents might choose the wrong name, room, or toys for the new baby as they did for him. He is reassured that if that happens, his sibling will be well supported, because they will have Aidan as their big brother. We have used this book because it offers a clear example of social transitions, using the phrase "transgender children". This book doesn't utilise metaphor or euphemisms as many others on the subject do, leaving practitioners better prepared to engage in open and direct discussions about gender identity.

Conversations with children

In my own practice there have been a range of conversations wherein a child has expressed in some way that they do not like or identify with their assigned gender. Three examples come to mind of this: one child who who would occasionally declare "I'm not a boy", another who told me they "don't want to be a girl", and another who had three different names (one typically given to girls and two typically to boys) depending on specific shirts they wore. In all instances, validation of the child's experience, even with a simple response of "that's okay", is a good starting point. Usually, this doesn't result in a particularly serious conversation as children play around with identity much more freely than adults so it's not often a particularly big deal. However, practitioners must be prepared to listen when a child does have more to say about their identity or is expressing something that could be dysphoria.

In the instance of the child telling me they don't want to be a girl, we did then have a longer conversation about what that meant to them. They told me they hated dresses and having long hair, that boys were just better and had cooler stuff. Of course, we did talk about how clothes, hair, toys, etc., didn't have to belong to a certain gender but it would have been unfair to dismiss their distress as just bias. My focus was on taking the time to really listen and making sure the child felt they were being seen as they are. This was very early in my career and I didn't necessarily feel as well equipped as I now would to ask what we could do to make them feel more comfortable in themself.

Cultivating a safe, affirming environment

Having clear policies in place regarding recognising and responding to transphobia is essential in upholding the Equality Act 2010. We have a duty to eliminate discrimination in our settings and this must be a priority in both policy and practice in order to be effective. It is not enough to declare early years settings as a "safe space for all" without setting and enforcing clear expectations on how discrimination will be handled.

It's uncommon in early years settings to have children use separate toilets or changing facilities based on gender. This is a positive thing as it negates the need for any child to feel unsure about where to go or that they are being made to use the "wrong" facilities. Suppose there are segregated facilities in your setting, for children or staff. In that case, the Equality Act 2010 protects the right of transgender people to use the facilities which align with their chosen gender.

Efforts made to help create a gender-inclusive environment and make changes to the way we utilise gendered language all contribute to making a space safer for trans and non-binary children. By consistently striving to centre inclusion, we signal that children are free to express themselves. Empathising with children is an essential part of the job especially as so many things are overwhelming and upsetting to young children in a way they wouldn't be to us. This empathy must extend to trans and non-binary children or any child expressing discomfort within themselves. The same gentle questioning we frequently practice when children are upset must extend to if a child is expressing distress about their gender.

Trans and non-binary parents and carers

It's important that our striving for inclusion extends to parents and carers both in how we welcome families looking to start their child with us and in how we maintain strong relationships throughout their child's time with us. Having a clearly stated ethos of inclusion on promotional materials like websites and posters can be a useful way to signal to trans and non-binary adults that they will be safe sending their child to you as long as your practice backs it up.

Early years practitioners must be able to build positive working relationships with a diverse range of adults in order to ensure effective communication and collaborative efforts to support children. Any refusal to engage with families based on aspects of identity such as gender identity is unacceptable. It's possible some practitioners may feel they lack the knowledge and understanding needed to provide adequate support; however, respecting someone and being able to engage constructively should not depend on your ability to directly relate to their lived experience. Prejudices impact our ability to effectively fulfil our safeguarding duties.

Concern or bigotry

A difficulty with transphobia, particularly surrounding trans and non-binary children, is that it is often framed as simply having "concerns". This is not a new concept by any means, and much of the current rhetoric surrounding trans people is identical to homophobic hate campaigns from previous decades. People are pulled in by the idea that a community they don't understand poses a threat and so hatred and fearmongering is actually about protection. The rhetoric that trans people are trying to turn children trans or that trans people aren't safe for children to be around has been a longstanding scare tactic against the LGBTQ+ community as a whole (Silin, 1997).

A common transphobic argument put forward as a concern includes statements like "well when I was little I identified as a dinosaur". This is highly unlikely to be comparable with the thoughts and feelings trans and non-binary children express when they tell us they identify a certain way. It's possible a child may want to be a dinosaur, but this is not the same as having a trans identity. Very few trans and non-binary people express their experience of gender as "wanting to be" a certain way but rather as already feeling a certain way within themselves that is at odds with their assigned sex. Perhaps it's also relevant to note that typically our response to a child telling us they are a dinosaur is not to say "no, you are a human" but rather to follow along and encourage their exploration.

"Concerns" from parents, carers, or even colleagues are not more important than trans and non-binary children's safety and wellbeing. It is important to facilitate discussions to prevent misinformation from turning people towards transphobia. However, we must do this whilst remembering that people's right to express their opinions does not mean their comments should go unchallenged.

Impact on mental health

Trans and non-binary people often have more mental health difficulties likely due to the impact of transphobia and gender dysphoria. However, early social transition can help to alleviate these difficulties and lead to better mental health outcomes.

A study of 73 socially transitioned trans children showed overall mental wellbeing to be high and levels of depression similar to that of cisgender children (Olson et al., 2016). A follow-up study on 116 socially transitioned trans children aged 6 to 14 years showed the same high levels of mental health and self-worth, concluding "these findings are in striking contrast to previous work with gender-nonconforming children who had not socially transitioned, which found very high rates of depression and anxiety" (Durwood et al., 2017, p. 1). A separate study focusing on trans children who use a chosen name found significantly lower depressive symptoms in those who were able to use their chosen name in educational settings as well as at home and with friends (Russell, S. T. et al, 2018). This demonstrates that the high rates of mental health difficulties we currently see faced by trans people are something we can change by teaching children about gender and supporting social transition.

In our practice, part of how we support this for better mental health outcomes is through the broader suggestions we've covered in other chapters such as not letting gendered expectations limit children's choices in settings, and taking steps to make children feel empowered in their identity. By already allowing children freedom to explore clothes and resources and take on different roles in their play we help alleviate the pressure on trans children to choose between hiding who they are or pushing against our expectations. We must also advocate for elements of social transition such as name or pronoun changes as the impact of these is powerful in helping children to feel accepted.

Reflection on trans childhood – R

I always felt hyper-aware of meeting people's expectations of what a girl was, even in my very early childhood, but it wasn't until my teens I really knew trans and other gender non-conforming people existed at all. The connection I felt to transness the moment I learned about it was such an immense relief.

I remember experiencing a lot of difficulty in forming friendships once I went into reception and in hindsight I think gender played a significant role in that. In my pre-school I was friends with boys and girls but in reception it felt like suddenly there was need to choose a side.

I struggle to imagine the positive impact seeing representation of different gender identities existence sooner could have had. Certainly, I would have felt less alone.

Policing gender

Transphobia necessitates creating strict definitions of "man" and "woman" with no room for compromise, something that historically has not been viewed as progressive. By advocating for segregated spaces based on assigned sex, rolling back protections for trans people, banning trans people from sports, etc., transphobes are essentially pushing for strict policing of bodies and expression. The current wave of transphobia is often framed as a "radical feminist" stance when in reality it's quite the opposite. For many years, women fought to be seen as more than just their reproductive systems and transphobia risks undoing that work.

As early years educators, we are supposed to be promoting acceptance, encouraging children to get along with one another and learn to empathise. This is one of the many reasons transphobia is inherently at odds with our aims and ethos. Teaching kindness and collaboration is incompatible with teaching children that society exists in two distinct opposite categories.

Pushing for strictly gendered sports also supports the idea that all women are inherently weaker/slower than all men. Recently even chess leagues have decided not to allow trans women to compete which clearly demonstrates a belief that women are also inherently less intelligent. Gendered categories only exist on the assumption gender is the most significant divider in ability, a message we most certainly aren't encouraged to pass on as educators.

The line between non-conforming and trans

There is an interesting question frequently posed regarding young people's understanding of their gender identity in particular: If gender is just a social construct or performance then how can what we like be an indicator of trans identity?

Whilst there's often overlap in people who don't "conform" to gender expectations and trans people, it's not entirely the same group. There will be girls who dislike every element of expression we associate with girls who still identify as girls and there will be boys who dislike every element of expression we associate with boys who still identify as boys.

As early years practitioners our focus must be on accepting that trans and non-binary people have a right to define themselves as such, and that we have the power to be either a positive or negative influence on their lives.

When you look back on your early childhood, is there a stand-out moment you now view as an indicator you were trans? – answers shared anonymously

I knew I was different but I didn't know how or why, just that I wasn't like the other boys. It felt like someone had taught them all the boy stuff and I'd been off sick and missed it and couldn't ever catch up. And I didn't want to. I wanted to be with the girls and I knew that wasn't allowed so I didn't tell anyone.

When I was four years old I became fascinated with the idea of being turned into a girl magically, though I didn't realize what it meant until I was much older.

I didn't understand why I couldn't wear any clothes, not just specifically clothes in the "girls section" in the store.

Everyone talks about how I was obsessed with the colour pink as a child. I never did particularly like pink, I just knew it made adults happy to see me in it.

My brother and I both had very gendered toy collections, which we both felt unsatisfied with and would combine to make much more interesting stories. I had a doll's house that often functioned as an army base for his action men.

I always knew. I don't actually have a singular memory because in my head it was obvious and I was pretty vocal about it early on.

Transgender history

Often when people are trying to push transphobia they frame transness and gender non-conformity as new concepts that are just fads we should ignore and they will go away. This is not true. There is consistent evidence of trans identities and other gender expansive ideas existing throughout human history in all sorts of ways.

In the UK specifically, looking back to the publication of Thomas Blount's *Glossographia* in 1656, the term "transfeminate" appeared, meaning "to turn from woman to man, or from one sex to another". The existence of a term referring to such an experience acts as proof that trans people existed and were understood enough to warrant defining. To look back even further, in a cataractonium in Catterick in North Yorkshire archaeologists uncovered the grave of a 4th-century AD woman called Gallus. "Born male", Gallus became a priestess of the goddess Cybele by self-castrating, cross-dressing, and taking a woman's role to demonstrate commitment to Cybele. Gallus was buried with jet jewellery amongst other female accessories suggesting a priestess's status, which implies acceptance by her community of her identity as a woman. Although we can't know how individuals from the past would identify based on current terminology, nor people's reasons for non-conformity and/or "transition", we do know that all throughout history there have been people who did not fit into one of two rigidly defined gender roles.

Understanding that trans people have always been around can be extremely useful when encountering transphobia in early years settings. Historically, there has been little to no education surrounding gender to young children and yet there have always been children who grew up trans, even in locations or periods of time where there is active criminalisation of gender non-conformity. This means that education, awareness, acceptance, and supporting early social transition cannot possibly be what makes people trans, it simply makes the lives of trans people easier.

Trans and non-binary staff

Currently, there is no data available on how many trans and non-binary people work in the early years sector as all current gender data has not included these categories. Some trans and non-binary people may also choose not to disclose their identity to avoid the risk of potential bias in hiring or dealing with discrimination in the workplace.

Any gender-related questions in applications or induction paperwork must be as inclusive as possible. The best way to do this is to allow people to write in their gender rather than utilising a finite list, as well as asking separately about pronouns. It can also be beneficial to have a separate space for name and legal name as these may not always be the same thing.

As so many early years settings are staffed exclusively by women, things like gendered dress codes are highly unlikely. In cases where there are different genders in the staff team, it is generally best practice to avoid different rules as these often promote stereotyping as well as potentially causing difficulties for trans and non-binary staff members.

Trans and non-binary staff may not want to be totally "out" at work, and this can mean different things. It may be that someone doesn't want parents or carers to know, it may be that someone doesn't want some or all of their colleagues to know. Nobody owes it to anyone to reveal their identity, and people's privacy must be protected for their safety and wellbeing. Providing comprehensive support to a trans or non-binary staff member may well include not talking about their identity and this must be respected.

Reflection on non-binary childhood – Chris

I was a child in the mid- to late 90s, and looking back now as someone who identifies as non-binary, feeling pressure to adhere to gender norms certainly affected me negatively.

I remember having a mermaid themed Polly Pocket (a little clamshell diorama toy) that I loved playing with, only to be told that I should be playing with the "boy" version of those toys when I had enthusiastically shown it to the other kids.

This has always stuck with me and, along with other things like needing to have a favourite football team, exemplifies the arbitrary boxes that I had to stay within to avoid exclusion by my peers. These gender-based rules didn't make sense to me, and at a formative age only served to limit how I was able to express myself, which is something I still struggle with to this day.

These experiences weren't uncommon then and probably aren't today either, though I want to hope that things are broadly more permissive and inclusive now. Regardless, I think anyone involved in a child's upbringing should help to foster an environment where that child is able to be curious and challenge norms that do not make sense to them.

Communicating with parents and carers

Another issue of debate is whether parents and carers should be informed when a child expresses that they are or may be trans. Some adults feel that practitioners have a duty to inform the child's family and that to not do that would be against safeguarding. The opposite is true, informing children's parents and carers of their trans (or potential trans) identity may be actively putting them in harm's way. Galop 2022 found that 44% of trans and non-binary people experienced abusive behaviour by a family member so this is a significant risk.

If a child confirms they want us to talk to their family, this can be a really positive opportunity to provide guidance and signpost to resources that will help them give their child the best support possible. There is a lot of misinformation out there, and a lot of discussions happening that don't centre trans people's wellbeing, so being able to make recommendations for seeking advice is essential. Parental support has been found to be a significant factor in quality of life for trans children, and knowledge and awareness are key to parental support (Barras and Jones, 2024).

There are charities such as Mermaids and Gendered Intelligence that provide a wealth of information and support including resources specifically tailored to parents and carers.

REFLECTION POINT

It's impossible to truly understand experiences outside of our own. Empathy is important and showing curiosity about each other's lived experiences is a great way to build connection. That being said, I don't want to treat the experience of being trans as a thought experiment. I think a more important reflection is on the current reality trans people experience, and where we ought to be positioned as early years practitioners. The negative impact of transphobia and dysphoria on wellbeing is severe. We know from studies and people sharing their lived experience that affirmative care and acceptance has a positive impact on wellbeing. Whether you understand trans identities or not is less important than whether you understand that you have a duty of care and a responsibility to reduce harm and promote wellbeing.

Conclusion

Increasing awareness of trans and non-binary people's existence must be accompanied by acceptance and progression of protection, otherwise the increased visibility can increase risk of harm. Whilst this can seem like a complex issue and sparks a lot of very heated debate the ultimate focus as practitioners, or anyone, has to be on supporting trans and non-binary children's wellbeing through affirmation and advocacy.

Further learning

The Dads (available on Netflix at time of writing) is a short documentary showing conversations between a group of fathers of trans children, as well as the father of the late Matthew Shepherd. They share stories of their journeys of acceptance and discuss the importance of supporting their children as well as forming their own support network with each other.

The Human Rights Watch report "I Want to Be Like Nature Made Me" (https://www.hrw.org/report/2017/07/25/i-want-be-nature-made -me/medically-unnecessary-surgeries-intersex-children-us) presents information from health professionals and intersex advocates on the lived experience of intersex people, including those who experienced cosmetic surgery as babies.

Growing Up Coy is a documentary following parents as they struggle to advocate for the rights of their trans daughter as she moves through education.

"Transgender Children Talk about Being Raised by Their Families" is a video by YouTube channel and news outlet "them" featuring trans children and their families from different backgrounds.

Before We Were Trans: A New History of Gender, a book by Dr Kit Heyam, provides a deeper understanding of gender variation through-out history, confirming that even though some terms may be new, there have always been people existing outside of the notion of a fixed gender binary.

Tammy Plunket's blog "The Joy of Raising Queer Kids" (https://blog .jkp.com/2022/06/the-joy-of-raising-queer-kids/) explains the ways in which being a parent to queer and trans children has been a source of joy for her.

References

Ainsworth, C. (2018) "Sex redefined: The idea of 2 sexes Is overly simplistic". *Scientific American*. Available at: https://www .scientificamerican.com/article/sex-redefined-the-idea-of-2-sexes -is-overly-simplistic1/

Anderson, A., Chilczuk, S., Nelson, K., Ruther, R., and Wall-Scheffler, C. (2023) "The myth of man the hunter: Women's contribution to the hunt across ethnographic contexts". *PLoS One*, 18(6), e0287101. https://doi.org/10.1371/journal.pone.0287101

Barras, A., and Jones, B. A. (2024, February 5) "'[He] can be supportive, but at times I feel he is ashamed of me': Understanding the relationship between parental support and quality of life amongst trans and gender diverse youth in the UK". *International Journal of*

Transgender Health, 25(1), 90–101. doi:10.1080/26895269.2023.22 86269. PMID: 38328592; PMCID: PMC10846468.

Blackless, M., Charuvastra, A., Derryck, A., Fausto-Sterling, A., Lauzanne, K., and Lee, E. (2000, March) "How sexually dimorphic are we? Review and synthesis". *American Journal of Human Biology*, 12(2), 151–166. doi:10.1002/(SICI)1520-6300(200003/04)12:2<151::AID-AJHB1>3.0.CO;2-F. PMID: 11534012.

Diamond, M, Beh, H. G, Richardson, W. S, Burns, J. A (2014) "Individuals with differences in sex development: Consult to Colombia Constitutional Court regarding sex and gender". *The Wisconsin Journal of Law, Gender & Society*, 29, 421–445.

Fausto-Sterling, A. (1993) "The five sexes". *The Sciences* (March/April) pp. 20–25.

Historic England (n.d.) "Trans and gender-nonconforming histories." *Historic England*. Available at: https://historicengland.org.uk /research/inclusive-heritage/lgbtq-heritage-project/trans-and -gender-nonconforming-histories/

Horton, C. (2023) "Euphoria: Trans children and experiences of prepubertal social transition". *Family Relations*, 72(4), 1890–1907. https://doi.org/10.1111/fare.12764

Galop (2022) *LGBT+ Experiences of Abuse from Family Members.* Available at: https://galop.org.uk/wp-content/uploads/2022/04/Galop-LGBT-Experiences-of-Abuse-from-Family-Members.pdf

Lukoff, K (2019). *When Aiden Became a Brother.* Lee & Low Books.

Olson KR, Durwood L, DeMeules M, McLaughlin KA. Mental Health of Transgender Children Who Are Supported in Their Identities. Pediatrics. 2016 Mar;137(3):e20153223. doi: 10.1542/peds.2015-3223. Epub 2016 Feb 26. Erratum in: Pediatrics. 2018 Aug;142(2):e20181436. doi: 10.1542/peds.2018-1436. PMID: 26921285; PMCID: PMC4771131.

Ruprecht, M. (2022) "Nearly all transgender kids stick with new identity 5 years later". *MedPageToday*. Available at: https://www .medpagetoday.com/endocrinology/generalendocrinology/98602

Russell, S. T., Pollitt, A. M., Li, G., and Grossman, A. H. (2018, October) "Chosen name use is linked to reduced depressive symptoms,

suicidal ideation, and suicidal behavior among transgender youth".
Journal of Adolescent Health, 63(4), 503–505. doi:10.1016/j.
jadohealth.2018.02.003. Epub 2018 Mar 30. PMID: 29609917;
PMCID: PMC6165713.

Silin, J. (1997) "The pervert in the classroom". In *Making a Place for
Pleasure in Early Childhood Education*, 214–234. New Haven: Yale
University Press.

The Black Nursery Manager (2019) "Intersectionality in the Early
Years setting". *Medium*. Available at: https://medium.com/@the
blacknurserymanager/in-any-early-years-setting-the-richness
-of-the-experiences-that-the-children-have-with-regards-to
-f3b029d7eae7

Zaliznyak, M., Bresee, C., and Garcia, M. M. (2020) "Age at first
experience of gender dysphoria among transgender adults seeking
gender-affirming surgery". *JAMA Netw Open*, 3(3), e201236.
doi:10.1001/jamanetworkopen.2020.1236. https://psychcentral.com
/disorders/gender-dysphoria-symptoms

Intersectionality

Intersectionality in gender-inclusive practice

The term "intersectionality" was coined by Kimberlé Crenshaw after initially being articulated by the Combahee River Collective, a Black feminist lesbian socialist organisation. It refers to the innate and inextricable entanglement between different forms of inequality, initially with a particular focus on the impact of misogyny and racism. "The intersectional experience is greater than the sum of racism and sexism, any analysis that does not take intersectionality into account cannot sufficiently address the particular manner in which Black women are subordinated" (Crenshaw, 1989).

Identities don't exist in a vacuum where neither impacts the experience of the other. It is therefore important to explore how other sources of either oppression or privilege interact with gender. In order to centre wellbeing, practitioners must be able to understand how multiple sources of inequality can impact social, emotional, and mental health (SEMH) and how to support children through that intersectional lens.

As early years practitioners, we want all children to feel able to achieve anything they want to. This is why understanding the different barriers different children will face and taking an intersectional approach is vital in recognising additional support and encouragement we can provide to give children the best possible start.

DOI: 10.4324/b23179-7

"Prism of difference"

A good way to think about intersectionality in relation to gender called the "prism of difference" was developed by feminist sociologists Maxine Baca Zinn, Pierrette Hondagneu-Sotelo, and Michael Messner.

> Imagine a ray of light – which to the naked eye, appears to be only one color – refracted through a prism onto a white wall. To the eye, the result is not an infinite, disorganized scatter of individual colors. Rather, the refracted light displays an order, a structure of relationships among the different colors – a rainbow. Similarly, we propose to use the "prism of difference" [...] to analyze a continuous spectrum of people, in order to show how gender is organized and experienced differently when refracted through the prism of sexual, racial/ethnic, social class, physical abilities, age and national citizenship differences.
>
> (2005)

The construct of gender and the limitations set by it are impacted by other aspects of identity. In order to support wellbeing we must develop an understanding of the variation in expectation of people who are the same gender but exist at different intersections of identity. Assuming that gender can be understood totally removed from any other factors means we may fail to recognise potential barriers to inclusive practice.

Gender around the world

The systems of gender are not the same across all cultures. There are positive differences, cultures that recognise a broader spectrum of gender and allow people the freedom to self-identify, and negative differences where assigned gender has an even greater impact on your opportunities and straying from expectation is punishable by law. Many cultures had much freer perceptions of gender before colonisation, and yet now there is a tendency to view those cultures as having fallen behind the Western cultures that took away their expansive views on gender in the first place. For example, Native Americans recognise an additional identity known as two-spirit. Two-Spirit individuals do not identify with either heterosexual orientation or cisgender identity. Two-Spirit people, historically, were respected spiritual leaders amongst their North American tribal nations. Indian texts from as early as 3000 years ago document a third gender, which has been connected to the hijras who have formed a category of third-gender or trans-feminine people on the Indian subcontinent since ancient times. In the Rigveda (from roughly 3500 years ago), it is said that before creation the world lacked all distinctions, including of sex and gender, a state ancient poets expressed with images like men with wombs or breasts (West, 2010, Nanda, 2014).

Most early years practitioners will work with families from a vast array of cultural backgrounds so we must be willing to seek further knowledge that may be relevant in offering all children and families the same support. Being able to talk to families and ask questions is important but relying on a parent or carer to offer all possible context with no attempt to learn independently can place an unnecessary burden and limit the information we receive.

As with anything that can impact wellbeing, our main duty is to the child. This can mean having to balance respecting a family's cultural or religious beliefs with maintaining best practices for inclusion and supporting wellbeing. Ultimately, we cannot compromise on fulfilling our duty to promote equality within our settings but we can facilitate respectful discussion and direct families towards useful resources.

Importance of intersectionality in practice

> As an Early Years workforce we are assisting and preparing children to be contributors to a fair, accepting and pleasant society it is therefore imperative that we examine Crenshaw's theory and heighten our awareness of precisely how it can directly impact the children that we work with every day.
>
> (Pemberton, 2019)

Understanding intersectionality is key to recognising and working to counter discrimination children face both within our settings and out in the world. If we are unable to fully recognise potential harm faced by children existing at different intersections of identity then we could be enabling or perpetuating that harm ourselves.

Considering intersectionality in practice could, for example, enable us to better understand the challenges a racially minoritised child who is going against the gender binary may face in terms of experiencing both racism and transphobia. If we only focus on one element of identity at a time, it's possible that discriminatory practices could remain unchallenged. Only through observing the interaction between different sources of oppression can we fully support children with a range of intersectional identities.

Resources

> If in their formative years, children do not see their realities reflected in the world around them or only see problematic representations mirrored back at them, the impact can be tremendously damaging. To redress imbalances in representation is not an act of charity but an act of necessity that benefits and enriches all of our realities.
>
> "Reflecting Realities", Centre for Literacy in Primary Education, 2018

Throughout this guide we have considered improving resources and how they are used with a strong focus on gender-inclusive practice in particular. However, a holistic view of diversity is necessary for creating a truly representative and inclusive environment. This means examining not only if individual identities are represented but also ensuring a range of intersections of identity are present within that. For example, when reflecting on the range of dolls in your setting you cannot just look for gender diversity, racial diversity, and disability representation as individual checklist points but must also consider whether all possible combinations of these identities are represented.

Craft supplies must give all children the opportunity to accurately reflect themselves and the people around them. In order to achieve this, consider whether the range of colours in crayons, pens, and pencils includes enough variety of possible skin tones. When it comes to things like paint or clay, ensure you have multiple options for skin tones and help children to create a "match" for themselves by mixing these together. The way you talk about these materials also impacts the way children use them. For example, if you have a wide variety but are still referring to one particular colour as "flesh" you are still reinforcing the idea of whiteness as the default.

It is incredibly common for early years books to use animals, fantasy creatures, or even typically inanimate objects as characters in place of humans. Whilst this does in some ways still allow for gender-inclusive stories, it presents a bigger issue in representing factors such as race or visible disabilities. These books can and do have value. Many of the most well-known and loved stories in early years do have animal main characters and that isn't going to suddenly change. The problem is when books without humans dominate early years bookshelves, we lose out on opportunities for comprehensive representation and inclusion and restrict potential learning in doing so. In some ways, having non-human characters may increase children's engagement as it provides a character any child can project onto. However, the importance of children seeing themselves and their experiences reflected cannot be overstated.

Books

Intersectionality has been considered in book recommendations throughout. Whilst representation in books is improving, there is still a long way to go to ensure the diversity we see in the real world is reflected in a range of stories. Often, books that do have a focus on inclusion lack the same popularity and availability as a lot of the more commonly seen stories reflecting a cisgender, non-disabled white nuclear family. This is why it's important to seek out specialist book-shops and support their business so that the demand for diverse stories is recognised and catered to by authors, illustrators, and publishers.

A New Chapter is an online bookshop that prioritises stocking a diverse range of books with representation of different minoritised identities. They have a dedicated early years section and provide sup-port to education settings that reach out to create book bundles suited to the kinds of representation they are seeking more of.

Taking intersectionality into account is essential to examining whether stories are perpetuating stereotypes. For example, when we think of a book that will empower girls, we typically imagine a girl being bold and confident. Whilst these are important, if we think of the context of Black girls often their depiction is as being "sassy" so it can actually be rarer and extremely valuable to have stories where a Black girl is allowed to be a more introspective character.

Book recommendations

Love Makes a Family *by Sophie Beer*

This book features playful examples of what love can consist of through a simple repeated sentence structure allowing for focus on images. The images feature a range of different family set-ups including diversity of gender expression and race. The simplicity of the story makes it suitable for the younger end of early years although the illustrations certainly make space for discussion with older children. It is a good resource to encourage conversation around family and what family means to different people.

All Are Welcome *by Alexandra Penfold and Suzanne Kaufman*

This book makes use of illustration to show a school environment filled with a diverse range of children all engaging with a range of activities together throughout their day. The text follows a pattern whilst explaining different aspects of the day and positive attributes of diversity whilst focusing on reinforcing that all are welcome. The text specifically addresses the strength of a diverse community in overcoming adversity in a way that is simple enough to be accessible with practitioner support. This book has potential to be used in a range of ways either focusing on the images or using the text to facilitate discussions around diversity.

REFLECTION POINT

Take some time to consider the multiple facets of your own identity. Which aspects might grant you privilege? Which aspects might mean you experience oppression? We have to understand our own place in the world before we can adequately support others. This doesn't mean passing on the responsibility of caring for children who don't share your identities but rather recognising there will be experiences you can never truly understand but will have to learn to help children and sometimes their families navigate.

Recognising our positions of privilege enables us to reflect on biases we may hold and take active steps to better educate ourselves and ensure these biases are not present in our practice, as well as recognise and address biases perpetuated by colleagues. Equally, recognising our sources of oppression allows us to reflect on the impact that has on our lives and actions we can take to minimise or counter harm caused to children and families that share our identifiers.

Finally, this concept also allows us to reflect on our own biases as to what kinds of families and communities can challenge heteronormativity. It is often assumed to be only white and middle-class families who wish to raise their children in more gender-sensitive ways. This is not true; however, the very perception can make it difficult for families from lower socio-economic backgrounds and/or racially non-white backgrounds to come forward and discuss such issues.

Recruitment

We've looked at the fact that, according to the 2018 Labour Survey, 92.6% of childcare workers were women. However, the lack of diversity in the early years education sector goes beyond just gender: the most prominent age band was 45–49, 86.9% were white, and at least 84% were born in England. According to the January 2020 "Schools, Pupils and Their Characteristics" report, 33.9% of primary-aged children were of minority ethnic backgrounds. The workforce is not reflective of the children in our care, meaning we are continuing to feed into a narrative of white authority rather than allowing children a wide range of role models.

Management in charge of recruitment have an additional duty to keep intersectionality in mind in creating a diverse staff team. "Diversity hire" is thrown around as a buzzword, and often there is an instinctive response of "shouldn't it go to whoever is best for the job?" This is problematic in that it is undercut with the assumption that the "diverse" candidate can't possibly have been the best. Furthermore, it's important to recognise lived experience of minoritised identifiers as a strength that will help improve the overall effectiveness of your team in providing the best care and education to a diverse range of children.

Often management will be trying to make applications inviting but without proper knowledge of how to do so. For example, having the question "do you need any reasonable adjustments" on your application isn't particularly useful for a lot of disabled candidates. You need to first provide information on the existing accessibility of your setting such as parking, information on stairs if there are any, breaks, and access to medication. There can be a reluctance to hire disabled staff due to uncertainty about safety working with children. This is where considering the team holistically is more important. Everyone has things they can and can't do whether that's due to disability or not; the essential thing is to be able to adapt to play to everyone's strengths and make sure possible gaps in ability are covered.

It's important that management demonstrate their understanding of intersectionality and lay out how policies relating to equity and equality are implemented. People are less likely to accept a job offer if they haven't got the sense they will be understood and protected. Often people can tell when others are seeing them as a token to collect or box to tick off in which case they are likely to turn down job offers and/or discourage other candidates who share their minoritised identifier from applying in the future.

Don't expect a new staff member to come in and take full responsibility for inclusion. It's possible to make it clear their input would be greatly valued as and when they feel able to offer it without putting all responsibility on them. Minoritised identities mean people are constantly expected to educate those around them whilst being endlessly patient and polite regardless of whether any effort is being put in by others. People aren't likely to stay in a job where they feel even more pressure to be doing this, especially when that shouldn't be a major part of their job role but rather a shared responsibility amongst all staff.

Broader representation

We've examined the positive impact on children of seeing themselves represented in our settings but we must also consider the importance of reflecting a full spectrum of human diversity regardless of whether that is reflected in any given cohort of children. After all, not every setting's location will be somewhere with a particularly diverse local community. In these cases, expansive representation is just as important as it serves the purpose of teaching children respect and empathy beyond their own experience.

Representation of physical disability is a particularly relevant example here. If the existence of visibly disabled people isn't normalised for young children it's easy for them to be confused by or discriminatory towards disabled people they come across throughout their lives. Mobility aids, hearing aids, and medical devices such as insulin pumps are some examples of disability aids we likely won't see in every cohort of children but still have the power to educate children about through comprehensive representation.

Sourcing diverse materials

Sometimes, seeking to diversify resources means looking beyond typical major brands. Whilst toy companies such as Mattel are consistently working to improve representation in their dolls, there are often smaller companies run by marginalised people creating resources that represent their identities. Funding is often inadequate across the sector, so it won't always be possible to invest in the best, specially made resources. However, that doesn't absolve practitioners of all responsibility to consider where available funds are being spent, and if intersectionality is as high a priority as it should be.

Making use of donated or second-hand resources is often a more accessible option. Your children's families can be included in this by identifying gaps in your provision and encouraging donations. Whilst it can be tokenistic to treat diverse resources as a checklist or to make judgements about which families may be able to donate which resources, welcoming families to be a part of positive changes you want to make towards inclusivity encourages collaborative progress rather than virtue signalling. Receptiveness to feedback from families is also important. It's easy to jump to defensiveness when people question whether your practice and resources demonstrate enough active understanding of intersectionality. However, often reflecting on feedback and seeking further relevant knowledge both independently and by maintaining open communication about how to do better is likely to lead to meaningful change.

Creating division

There is sometimes concern that in observing the intersections of identity which exist in a particular group we are creating an unnecessary division. The concern comes from a position of privilege wherein it's assumed by not acknowledging and accounting for potential sources of oppression and privilege we somehow create equality. People who experience discrimination are always aware of these divisions in any space as a matter both of safety and of connection. We feel safer with people who we know face similar oppression to our own and are wary of people who typically uphold oppressive systems.

The reality is that these divisions already exist. All aspects of our identity and circumstances have the ability to impact our opportunities, and pretending this isn't the case means those systems will just continue to exist. Whilst the "we see everyone the same here" mentality feels well-meaning, if we refuse to acknowledge differences we can't possibly notice patterns in the way different children are treated.

Facing one source of discrimination doesn't exempt you from perpetuating other kinds or even having internalised bigoted beliefs about your own identity. Sometimes this can feel like protection by aligning yourself with oppressors so that they aren't targeting you. However, there is far more power in banding together in active allyship with each other than there could ever be in trying to separate yourself in the hopes of being left alone.

Intersectionality in early childhood research

Whilst there are increasing studies into the impact minoritised identities have on children's development in early childhood, and some of these do consider multiple facets of identity, there are few studies which truly take intersectionality into account.

As Burman (2013, 234) states: "while intersectionality now features within discussions of childhood, it has yet to figure as a topic of analytical debate, perhaps because the concept and debate has largely arisen within feminist studies". A focus on intersectionality in studies going forwards is essential in ensuring we first fully understand the development impact so that we are able to establish best practice for minimising and counteracting that impact within our settings.

Allyship

The word "allyship" is one that often gets misused as simply not being actively discriminatory. However, allyship must be seen as an active process in order to achieve inclusive practice. By claiming ally as an identity we risk ignoring our potential to cause harm.

Not only is it important to practise active allyship as practitioners, it's important we start children on their path of active allyship too. This can look like allowing children's instinctive spark of defiance that makes them ask why you've told them to do something. (If you can't explain what you've said then you probably didn't need to say it!) Teaching compliance is outdated and unhelpful – I don't want children to listen to me just because they think they have to, I want them to listen to me because I'm making sense and, more importantly, because I listen to them. We need people who question policy, who look at the way things are and ask if it really has to be that way, if we want to keep moving forwards as a society.

An often overlooked aspect of allyship is community engagement. Raising awareness, organising or supporting fundraisers can be effective ways to contribute to reducing harm cause by discrimination. Early years settings can strive to establish themselves as part of their local community through collaborating with local charities or organisations to provide mutually beneficial opportunities and encourage engagement with families.

REFLECTION POINT

Do you consider yourself an ally to communities you are not a part of? If you do, can you think of actions you have taken as part of this allyship? When you hear discriminatory comments, do you step in every time?

Think about how allyship shows up in your setting. Are there opportunities for outreach being missed? Do you avoid conversations about discrimination with colleagues, children, and families or do you make the most of these conversations? It won't always feel comfortable, but it's essential that our values are present in practice, not just in theory.

Gender and neurodivergence

Boys are more likely to be recognised as diagnosed as neurodivergent. For example, although we know that people of all genders can be autistic, autism is still diagnosed between three and four times more often in boys compared to girls (Loomes et al., 2017). There have been different explanations offered for this over time, such as thinking boys genuinely are more likely to be neurodivergent or that girls present a totally different set of traits. It's certainly true that boys have historically been overrepresented in research on neurodivergence, so the suggestion girls may present different traits comes from the lack of sufficiently mixed candidates in research that contributes to diagnostic criteria.

Often in early years, neurodivergent children won't have a diagnosis, even if professionals and/or guardians have a reasonable idea about which terms might be appropriate. This is partly because neurodivergent traits can become more or less observable at different ages and in different environments. For example, a child that thrives in a freeflow nursery may struggle once they reach more structured key stages whilst another may find freeflow overwhelming and have a need to establish a firmer routine. Diagnosis at any point is difficult to obtain if a person is "on track" academically. Another reason is that referrals for diagnostic tests are dependent on both the child's guardian and their general practitioner (GP) being on board, which unfortunately doesn't always happen. In fact, sometimes councils will cap the number of diagnoses in order to save money, so even with observable traits, a supportive guardian, and a GP willing to refer, the correct diagnosis isn't necessarily given. Gender is an additional barrier to both diagnoses and recognition of neurodivergent traits by early years professionals or parents and carers.

This is why it is essential in early years to be aware of the wide range of traits within the special educational needs and disabilities (SEND) remit and examine our own bias regarding how we perceive these traits in different genders so that we can recognise what a child needs help with and provide appropriate support to the child and advice to parents and carers. It is important to recognise signs beyond tracking behind chronological age, and to be sensitive to the fact that behaviour a practitioner might think is "challenging" can often mean children are struggling with something, even if their academic progress is on track. Whether a child has a diagnosis or not, it is essential to focus on the individual needs of the child. Even solely looking at Autism, the current Diagnostic Statistical Manual's (DSM V) diagnostic label of Autistic Spectrum Disorder replaced what were formerly four separate diagnoses (autistic disorder, Asperger's disorder, childhood disintegrative disorder, and pervasive developmental disorder not otherwise specified). This means that the range of traits is so broad that two individuals who have the exact same diagnosis on paper could have little to no crossover, regardless of whether they are the same gender or not. Alternatively, two people who describe their experiences very similarly may get different diagnoses due to specific criteria or even just their doctors' opinions. Formal diagnoses do give us some insight into a child's needs, but this doesn't make an individual assessment of needs any less important. An ongoing effort needs to be made to recognise where a child needs support, where they are making progress, what is interesting to them, and what their vehicle for learning is. This is the only way we can truly centre the individual: through gaining as much insight as we can into who they are as a person and how their additional needs fit into that.

Gender and sexuality

Sexuality has been brought up in other chapters as society's gender roles are inextricable from the ultimate expectation that everyone must find someone of the "opposite" gender to become a family. This is often referred to as "heteronormativity" or "cisheteronormativity".

The LGBTQ+ community includes people whose sexuality and/or gender identity diverges from heterosexual and cisgender, as a lot of the discrimination faced has the same premise. The struggles faced by people of different identities within the community are not identical but we all experience the same "othering" so standing together as a community to support each other and advocate for change is essential.

Much like with gender identity, there can be pushback on talking to young children about sexuality due to concerns it is inappropriate. The perceived risks in enabling children to learn about LGBTQ+ identities must be reconciled with the risks of not doing so; a smoothing over of the ways in which children experience and learn about sexualities leaves them in ignorance surrounding this topic, and in fact perpetuates heteronormativity. Conservative MP Esther McVey's recent statement that parents should have the choice to remove their children from lessons about LGBTQ+ relationships in schools until they are 16 years old is a concrete example of the logic of childhood innocence (Allegretti, 2019). Being cisgender and heterosexual is positioned as the default identity formation until a choice is made otherwise and children are seen as more in need of safety over and above the granting of more liberties.

Gender and race

There is a vast range of intersections of gender and race that greatly impact how someone is perceived by society. Westernised ideals of gender are typically focused on white people so discrimination based on gender is inherently worse when racism is an additional factor as people of colour are less likely to be perceived as successfully meeting gendered expectations.

A specific well-documented example of the way gender bias and racism interact in early years is known as the adultification of Black girls. Societal expectations of children vary based on gender and race, and for Black girls this often means an expectation of maturity that interrupts their opportunity to fully experience childhood. This harmful idea can lead to adults offering less care and being less nurturing to Black girls which then necessitates an independence that's weaponised as evidence of maturity.

Writing for the Black Feminist Collective, Oluwademilade Ogunlade stated that "actionable steps appear simple but they change big things for small people. They include letting little Black girls cry, throw tantrums, ask questions, try unique hobbies, make temporary physical changes" (2023). As early years practitioners we must ensure we value all children's right to exist as children, engaging with the full range of experiences that can encompass in our settings. Awareness of commonly held biases such as the adultification of Black girls needs to be backed up by both self-reflection and a willingness to challenge others.

Conclusion

Intersectionality is a vast and complex topic, but the importance of taking the time to learn in order to examine and make changes to our own practice cannot be overstated. The examples provided in this chapter are just a few of the many ways in which gender interacts with other elements of identity to form sources of oppression that cannot be neatly separated and handled independently. Identifying specific areas to focus on for professional development is necessary in ensuring continued improvement but this must always be backed up by consideration through an intersectional lens.

Further learning

The map of gender-diverse cultures (https://www.pbs.org/independentlens/content/two-spirits_map-html/) is an interactive tool to learn more about gender in different cultures.

Kimberlé Crenshaw's TED talk "The Urgency of Intersectionality" explains the importance of intersectionality and the impact of only addressing individual sources of oppression.

Liz Pemberton (https://www.theblacknurserymanager.com) has written about intersectionality and offers different training options with a focus on anti-racism.

Kerry Murphy (https://www.eyfs4me.com) has multiple books predominantly aimed at helping practitioners support neurodivergent children and offers training.

Shaddai Tembo (https://www.criticalearlyyears.org) is a lecturer, writer, speaker and trainer with a strong focus on addressing societal issues in early years.

References

Allegretti, A. (2019) Esther McVey under fire for defending parents pulling children out of same-sex relationship classes. *Sky News.* Available at: https://news.sky.com/story/esther-mcvey-under-fire-for-defending-parents-pulling-children-out-of-same-sex-relationship-classes-11731759

Burman, E. 2013. "Conceptual resources for questioning 'child as educator'." *Studies in Philosophy and Education 32*(3): 229–243.

Crenshaw, K. (1989) "Demarginalizing the intersection of race and sex: A black feminist critique of antidiscrimination doctrine, feminist theory and antiracist politics". https://chicagounbound.uchicago.edu/cgi/viewcontent.cgi?article=1052&context=uclf

Konstantoni, K., and Emejulu, A. (2017) "When intersectionality met childhood studies: The dilemmas of a travelling concept". *Children's Geographies*, 15(1), 6–22. https://doi.org/10.1080/14733285.2016.1249824

Nanda, Serena (2014) *Gender Diversity* (2014, ISBN 147861546X), p. 28.Chicago, Waveland Pr Inc.

Ogunlade, O. (2023) "Red lips and red tips: Thoughts on the adultification of black girls". https://blackfeministcollective.com/2023/05/12/red-lips-and-red-tips-thoughts-on-the-adultification-of-black-girls/

Pemberton, L. (2019) "Intersectionality in the early years setting". https://medium.com/@theblacknurserymanager/in-any-early-years-setting-the-richness-of-the-experiences-that-the-children-have-with-regards-to-f3b029d7eae7

The Trans Language Primer (n.d.) "Two-Spirit (2spirit)". Available at: https://translanguageprimer.com/two-spirit/

West, Barbara A. (2010) *Encyclopedia of the Peoples of Asia and Oceania*, pp. 277–278. New York, Facts On File Inc

Zinn, M. B, Hondagneu-Sotelo, P, Messner, M. A, (2005) "Gender through the prism of difference". Oxford University Press.

Closing remarks

Closing remarks

My years of experience in early years settings have led to a greater understanding of the role education plays in discrimination, and as such the role it can play in overcoming that. I have found that caring for and educating children must also be accompanied by consistently advocating for their needs in order to improve outcomes. The early years workforce is overworked and underappreciated and that is something that urgently needs to change in order to make full use of that opportunity to combat oppression through our practice. Being a part of shaping young lives is truly a privilege and I believe it to be one of the most important jobs in terms of overall impact on society. However, the current system means many people are unable to continue that privilege due to low wages, high stress, and lack of adequate support.

I have also found that there is an inherent activism to early years practice that can be underutilised if it isn't acknowledged. Whilst it's certainly not the only action to take, providing children with better care and education is one of the most effective ways to ensure a future where there is much broader acceptance of difference and significantly less bigotry and discrimination. Imparting an ethos of understanding and acceptance as well as a strong sense of justice is how we help to ensure future generations see continued progression of human rights and quality of life.

Self-reflection will always be at the heart of best practice, though the fast pace and high expectations we have to deal with as early years practitioners can make it hard to find the time for this. Things like excessive paperwork and continuously preparing for Ofsted can mean we lose sight of centring our ability to hone our practice through making space to consider the impact we have and how we can address any issues to maximise the positive role we play in children's development. The overwhelming majority of practitioners are entirely well-meaning but are held back by not having the time and resources to adequately address their individual bias as well as the presence of bias in their settings.

Whilst gender as a concept can be a hot topic of debate, it's important to humanise the impact this has on our lives. It's easy to argue when we are externalising gendered hypotheticals rather than grounding conversation surrounding discrimination and harm in reality by reminding ourselves and each other that this harm is experienced by real people and there are actions we can all take to reduce that. We are all unique, and children must be allowed to explore and enjoy their uniqueness and have this not just respected but celebrated by the adults in their lives. Although we may never be able to truly understand gender as experienced by others, our empathy and willingness to strive for a better future can act as guiding forces in our journey to achieve inclusive practice.

Final reflection point

What does your work as an early years practitioner mean to you? The day-to-day functions of the job may consist of seemingly trivial things like nappies and running around the garden, but everything we do has the ability to impact how the children in our care move through the world as they grow. Our impact on them influences their impact on the world.

What do you hope is different for the children in your care when they grow up? It can be difficult to carve out space for hope when so much of the noise we hear is about awful things happening and the subsequent waves of anger, distress, and hatred that causes. We mustn't ignore these things, but we must carry with us the faith that things can get better. Maybe your actions won't change the whole world overnight but that doesn't negate the value of the difference each person can make to the lives of those around them.

Glossary

Glossary

Assigned sex

This refers to the assignment of male or female based on visual examination at birth.

Cisgender (cis)

A term that describes someone whose gender identity aligns with the sex the person was assigned at birth.

Gender

Gender can be understood as a social system of practices, norms, and expectations within society that constitute and characterise people as different in socially significant ways, typically based upon masculinity and femininity.

Heteronormativity/cisheteronormativity

A concept used to describe practices that socially exclude or marginalise non-heterosexual people and preserve heterosexuality as the norm, perpetuating that in society there are two distinct genders and relationships should be between one person of each gender.

Intersex

Intersex people are born with characteristics that do not fit neatly into typical definitions of male or female. Very few countries offer legal recognition of intersex babies and so in the vast majority of cases they are still assigned as male or female.

LGBTQ+

An umbrella term to refer to all current and future minoritised sexual orientations and gender identities, with the plus symbol used as a proxy to represent both the wide variety of established genders and orientations beyond the initialism and those who are part of the community but have a more fluid sense of identity and do not necessarily feel drawn to particular labels. (Some people prefer alternative acronyms, such as LGBTQIA+ or 2SLGBTQI+, which incorporate identities often forgotten in conversations about the community.)

Non-binary

A term that describes someone whose gender identity sits outside of the gender binary system, which itself refers to the belief that there are only two gender identities.

Sexual orientation

A term used to refer to attraction or desire toward others in relation to gender.

Transgender (trans)

A term that describes someone whose gender identity does not align with the sex the person was assigned at birth.

Transphobia

Discrimination or prejudice against trans people.

Index

T - #0109 - 051224 - C136 - 210/148/6 - PB - 9781032367842 - Matt Lamination